A Christian Counselor's Primer On...

For helping those who struggle with.....

Anger & Rage

A series of Resource Manuals for Counselors, Pastors, Teachers, Altar Workers, & all those who serve to comfort and equip the Body of Christ.

Written by
Debbye Graafsma, bcpc

Book One

Awakened!!
Awakened to Grow
Counsel. Classes. Retreats
awakenedtogrow.com

DISCLAIMER

The lesson materials contained in this primer notebook are provided for informational purposes only. These materials, and any or all accompanying materials published by the author, are not in any way intended to diagnose, treat, or evaluate mental illness; nor are they a substitute for professional counseling and care. Those who suffer from the difficulties covered in "A Christian Counselor's Primer On ..." series of handbooks should seek additional counsel for their unique situation. Optimally, the materials should be worked through with a trained professional counselor.

The information contained herein is provided for educational purposes only. The user assumes all risks. Debbye Graafsma, and Awakened to Grow, and their affiliates deny responsibility for any and all misuses of the information provided.

Awakened to Grow Ministries
P.O. Box 546
Indian Trail, NC 28079
Website: awakenedtogrow.com

A Christian Counselor's Primer on Anger and Rage; A series of resources for those who help others...
Book 1 (ISBN 978-0-9852680-6-0)

©2014 Debbye Graafsma, Awakened to Grow. No portion of this manuscript, nor its accompanying materials may be reproduced or stored by any means or in any format without the written expressed consent of the owners.

A Christian Counselor's Primer on...Anger and Rage

Table of Contents

Introduction -- 7

Section One.

    Basic Principles of Growth and Healing--- 9

Section Two.

    Facts about Anger--19

Section Three.

    The Sources of Anger--29

Section Four.

    The Counselor's Role in Helping Those Who Struggle with Anger--------------43

    Self-Assessments and Discovery materials --------------------------------------- 52

Section Five.

    Required Choices to Heal -- 67

Section Six.

    The Bible on Anger-- 71

Section Seven.

    Scriptural Prayer and Supportive Materials.-------------------------------------81

Introduction One
(Books 1-4)

Dear Fellow Servant,

If you are reading this, you are either considering purchasing this little hand-book or, have already purchased it... Perhaps you are deliberating how you will incorporate it into your ministry or counseling practice. It is my hope that the information contained here will become a tool, to enable and equip you to more effectively hear and Holy Spirit when it comes to helping others. Not only that; but it is my goal to make your efforts even more fruitful, by providing you with Biblical background and lessons to accompany counseling materials.

Each book in this series: "A Christian Counselor's Primer on...." contains current information relevant to its subject, suggested methods of treatment, as well as a series of charts on its topic that I have developed over the past twenty years in private pastoral counseling practice. Over this period of time, I have found my clients respond more positively when I chart out the truths regarding spiritual and emotional conditions. Doing this allows a person to identify their own experience as it relates to the picture presented to them. We then discuss and learn in conversational one-on-one discipling.

Additionally, I have also developed self-assessments and questionnaires for my clients, in order to aid and speed individual discovery. I have included those assessments and/or questionnaires in these hand-books as they relate to the subjects at hand.

At the end of each hand-book are suggested reading lists for you, the counselor, allowing further study, as well as for the client, allowing personal growth and development.

In Christian circles, it is sometimes too easy to give "pat" answers, or "quick fixes," without seeing actual healing and growth take place in the lives of those we are seeking to serve. Such situations render the client feeling inept, or worse, without enough "faith" to find solution. The fact that you are looking at this booklet exempts you from the circles in which those damaging office visits occur. Thank you for your desire to serve: helping and bringing healing to those who are wounded.

That being said, please allow me take a couple of moments to encourage you.

The ministry of providing a safe place for counsel is a vital one. So much brokenness exists in our society today; so much pain. And yet, only one person out of every four people who are referred to a counseling office will actually make the call and follow-through to keep the appointment. And, of those in that 25 percentile, only around half will actually commit to applying the training they receive in sessions, realizing change and growth. That means that together, as counselors, all of us have about a 13% chance of helping anyone! Believe it or not, that is really good news! After all, just one transformed life can change the world!!

Imagine. What could happen if thirteen out of every one hundred people in your sphere of influence became impassioned and empowered to grow, not only emotionally, but spiritually as well?

Years ago, General Motors' famed inventor and head of research, Charles Kettering, made a very wise declaration in describing how his department approached the concept of designing need-meeting vehicles. He said, "A problem well-defined is half-solved." Not only is this statement true when it comes to designing cars, but it is also true when it comes to the process of learning to choose well in living.

When a client can see the "why" of their struggle in growth and healing, they are more than half-way to discovering the repentant heart and desire to change they need to acquire more healing and therefore, health in their Christian Walk! An encounter with God is then just steps away! Hopefully, using the materials contained here will make than encounter a reality!

In the beginning of each volume, I explain a little about how the Father God's principles of healing work when it comes to emotional healing and spiritual development; with each volume building on the prior volume's teaching. Hopefully, this will help you to discover a sense of empowerment and personal mission. After all, that's why each of us began in this helping ministry......

It is my hope to help you and bless you!

Blessings!

Debbye Graafsma, M.Div., D.Min., bcpc
Awakened to Grow Ministries

Section One.
Basic Principles of Growth and Healing

(for Books 1-4; Jesus' parable, "The Sower and the Soil")

There are four volumes in the "A Christian Counselor's Primer on...." series of handbooks. Within each volume are five manuals, or "quick-study" texts, designed to provide an overview of the materials presented. For volume one, books 1-5, we will consider the first parable Jesus Christ told during His ministry on earth: "The Sower and the Soil" as a springboard for basic understanding.

There is such hope and encouragement to be drawn from this parable. And the fact that it was the first parable Jesus told, also gives us a glimpse of the attitude of Abba Father towards us – even when we are in the worst of conditions.

The idea of healing the hearts of men and women began with Jesus. Continually, throughout His ministry on earth, our God spoke to the very roots and cause of the Pain and dysfunction each of us carry: our baggage, if you will. It is His method to say, "You have heard it said – but *I say to you....*" And then He finishes the statement with something that changes the entire perspective on whatever subject He was speaking.

Jesus came to heal. Jesus came to restore. Jesus came to redeem and rebuild those things lost and broken; those parts of us deemed as beyond repair.

The parable of the Sower is particularly precious in my own life, because the Holy Spirit used it in my own life to challenge my personal depth meter when it comes to emotional and spiritual development.

And let me just say this as we begin: Spiritual development and Emotional maturity cannot be separated. It is impossible to become a healthy, emotionally congruent individual, without finding ourselves at a crossroads of sorts. What will I do with the spiritual issues that stir in my soul when I decide I want to experience "more?" What answers will I allow to pervade and influence my mind and heart? By the same token, personal spiritual development cannot become a reality, unless I choose to yield yet again to the Holy Spirit of the Living God, and allow Him to challenge, confront, and change the attitudes and patterns of my dysfunctional past; allow Him to mold and form on deeper and deeper core levels, His nature and Personality within me....

Jesus Christ was a master Storyteller. In imparting Life-truths, He would weave a story that people related to and were fascinated by. The Sower and the Soil is one of my favorites. Jesus explained this particular parable as being about the human heart; or what we would describe the soul. *(The human soul, is comprised of our mind, will and emotions; what we think, choose and feel.)*

Before we go to the parable, let me share a couple of charts with you, that I hope will serve you well in your desire to help others. When I first began counseling, these were some of the first I developed, and I find I use each of them at least once a day, even now.

The first chart, is the description of the Levels of Relationship and Communication. This is a basic chart that defines the difference between IQ, Intelligence Quotient, and EQ, Emotional Quotient. Emotional Quotient, or Emotional Intelligence, as it is being referred to these days, has to do with one's ability to relate to other people. EQ has to do with the deeper levels of living we all experience with the people we are closest to in relationships.

Jesus referred to the Emotional Quotient, as the "Heart of Man."

Please consider the IQ/EQ chart below.

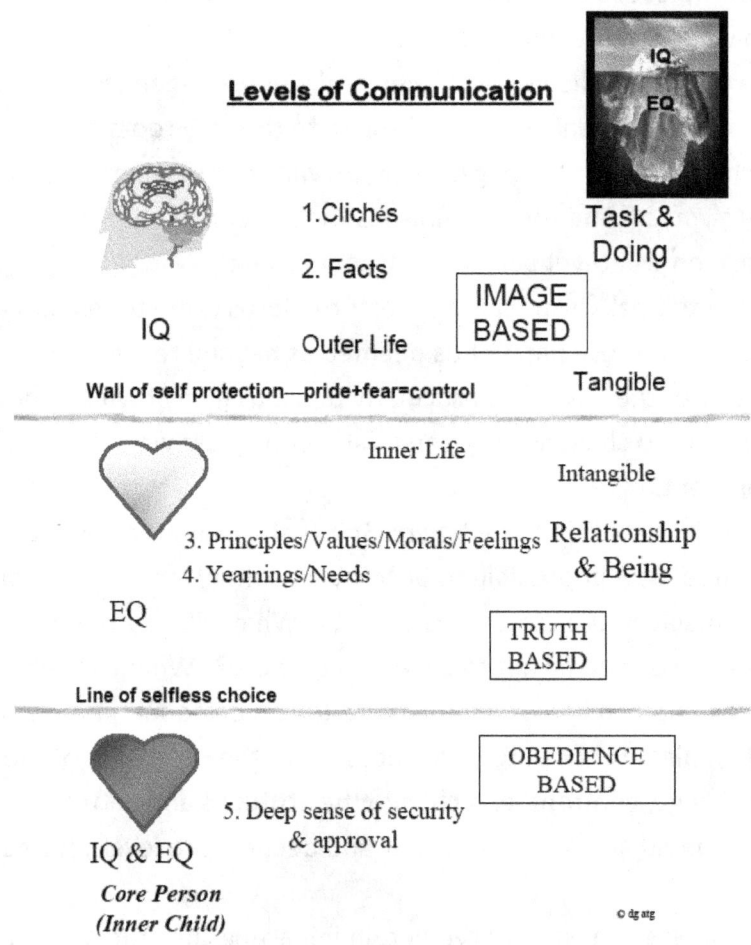

When we study this chart, we discover the differing depths of relationship each of us experience in our lives.

Level 1 = Cliches   These are the people we meet once on an elevator, or in a crowded room, and make **surface-level conversation** with, experiencing no fear or sense of risk.

Level 2= Facts   These are the relationships we encounter in our lives who require **a little more expenditure from us – but still without emotional impartation.** For example, when we are in school, we must memorize and repeat the facts. How well we remember many of the facts determines our Intelligence Quotient. (That is, "are we intelligent, able to apply the facts?" Also, "how well do our life achievements 'stack up' against others' lives, etc.")

A life lived on only levels 1 and 2 will be image based, success oriented, shallow in nature, and dependent upon performance orientation.

Between levels 2 and 3, there exists a Wall of Self-Protection. The wall is comprised of Pride and/or Fear. Simply put, Fear + Pride = Control. Most of us construct our personal wall in pre-puberty, or just after, depending upon the comparisons we make between our "nest" and the "nests" of those in our friendship circle, and how our own sense of "normal" compares to the "normal" of our friends and acquaintances.

Level 3 =   A *man* will experience Level 3 of relationships when he is able to determine his personal **principles and values,** and express them to his companions. A *woman* will experience Level 3 in relationships when she is able to express her **morals and feelings** to her companions. There are reasons for these differences in approaching this level of relationship differently; gender being the main reason.

Level 4 =   **Yearnings and needs** are what make up the deepest part of our being. In this level, we are able to share our hopes and dreams as they relate to our future. These are the deepest perceived needs we carry; many times without expression.

A life lived incorporating levels 3 and 4 into daily experience, will manifest the Personhood of a well-bonded individual. Such a person has chosen to cease trying to "hold to the image" of who he or she believes must be portrayed in day to day living.

However, what actually fuels, or gives power to, the Emotional Quotient levels of our lives is the substance of Truth. In places where we have learned to believe our experiences as being the source of Truth, we will develop broken trust and an inability to relate to others in a healthy way. (This is something we all do.)

When we become believers in Christ, the Holy Spirit begins the process of personal transformation; bringing comfort, healing, change and growth. In the midst of this maturation, there comes a point in the life of every believer when he or she is confronted with the realization of the disparities and contrasts between what our experiences and taught us to be true, and the Truth of God's Word.

If a person chooses to cling to the perceptions he or she has always believed; the person's own conclusions of "truth;" then the processes of emotional development and spiritual maturation cease. Sadly, when this type of refusal to the Spirit's formation occurs, any future discoveries the believer receives will be tainted by that refusal; influenced by elements of fear and legalism.

In contrast, when a believer is willing to take the risk of trusting God for their emotional development, the Holy Spirit (the Helper and Teacher) continues the process of healthy emotional and spiritual development by breathing courage into the soul. He then will confront the believer with the need to exchange those inward perceptions of "truth" for Abba Father's Truth. When our "truth," or perception, is traded for God the Father's Truth, the Bible becomes a template learning how to live the life of a believer. At that point of growth, the Word of God becomes real to us; more than mental assent.

At that point, *His Truth* becomes voluntarily traded for *our truth*. *His Truth* is durable, unshakable, and trustworthy.

Then, as we continue our lives in Jesus Christ, at some future point of our development, we each must come to another place of choosing. This second choice presents us with as question. Will we allow the Holy Spirit to deepen our resolve and obedience with God?

This is the choice to move forward without looking back. It is at this point we discover that we are disciples of Jesus Christ. This second choice, or "wall," if you will, is the fear which confronts us when we seek to give our lives away, or invest our efforts into a cause that will benefit others. When the choice towards discipleship is make, we become willing to offer something of ourselves to God, and to others, simply for the common good. We do it with a sense of purpose and fulfillment, and it is an offering that comes from deep within.

This deepest part of us, I refer to as the Core, or Inner Child.

Now, let's take a look at how those levels of communication affect our personal relationships.

The journey of the Christian life is one that takes us inward, as well as one that focuses our intentions outward. The inward journey of personal Discovery and Empowerment requires the confronting of imprinting, pain and experiences with cause us to be malformed in our emotional growth and development. This is what only the Creator can re-imprint and heal. After all, God is the only Perfect Parent. The outward journey determines the direction of our personal development. It also maintains our balance. In this journey, the Holy Spirit teaches us how to express His care and love for others – without pretense or fear, as disciples of the Living God.

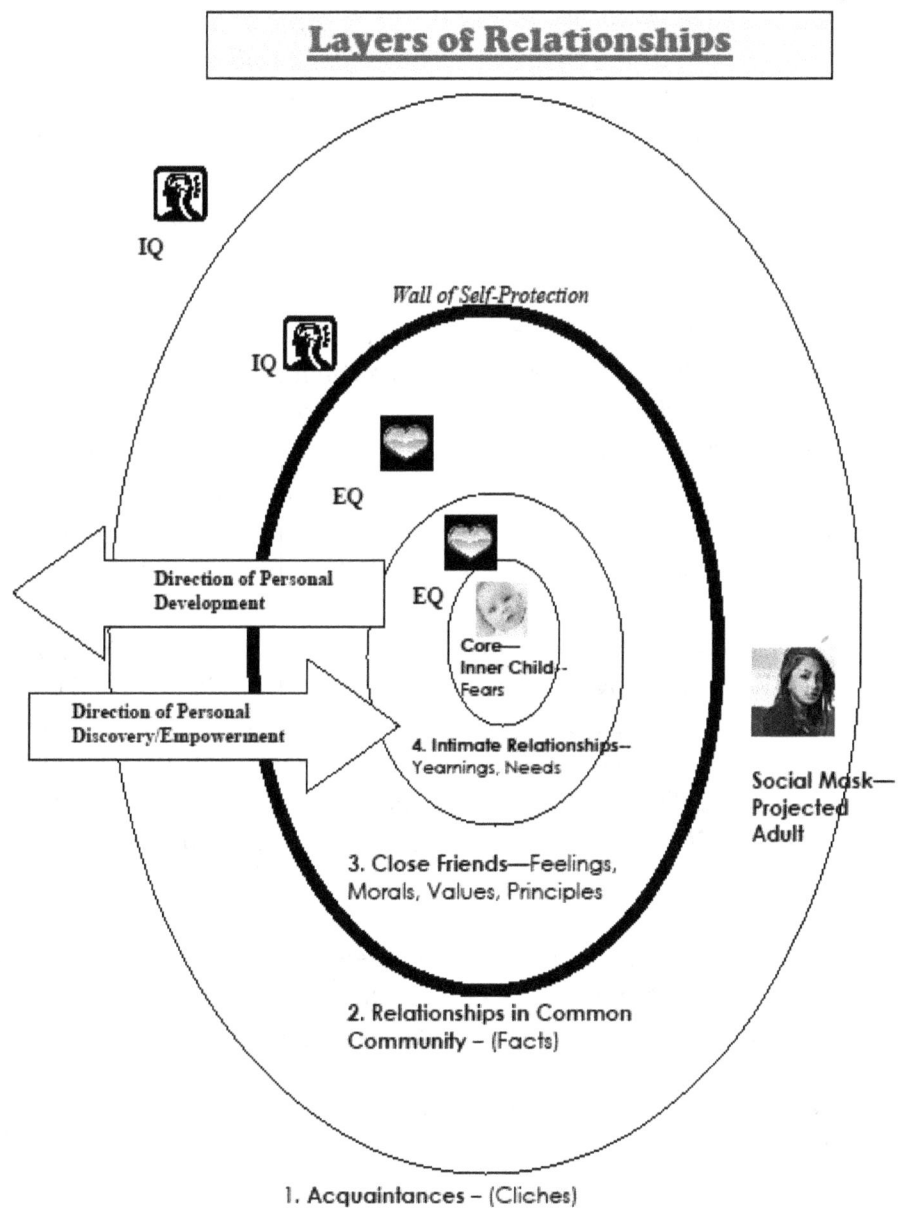

Jesus continually referred to this growth and discovery process. In Matthew 13, our Savior told a parable about a sower, his seed, and the soil.

"That day Jesus went out of the house and was sitting by the sea. And large crowds gathered to Him, so He got into a boat and sat down, and the whole crowd was standing on the beach. And He spoke many things to them in parables, saying, "Behold, the sower went out to sow; and as he sowed, some seeds fell beside the road, and the birds came and ate them up. Others fell on the rocky places, where they did not have much soil; and immediately they sprang up, because they had no depth of soil. But when the sun had risen, they were scorched; and because they had no root, they withered away. Others fell among the thorns, and the thorns came up and choked them out. And others fell on the good soil and yielded a crop, some a hundredfold, some sixty, and some thirty. He who has ears, let him hear.

And the disciples came and said to Him, "Why do You speak to them in parables?" Jesus answered them, "To you it has been granted to know the mysteries of the kingdom of heaven, but to them it has not been granted. For whoever has, to him more shall be given, and he will have an abundance; but whoever does not have, even what he has shall be taken away from him. Therefore I speak to them in parables; because while seeing they do not see, and while hearing they do not hear, nor do they understand.

In their case the prophecy of Isaiah is being fulfilled, which says, YOU WILL KEEP ON HEARING, BUT WILL NOT UNDERSTAND; YOU WILL KEEP ON SEEING, BUT WILL NOT PERCEIVE; FOR THE HEART OF THIS PEOPLE HAS BECOME DULL, WITH THEIR EARS THEY SCARCELY HEAR, AND THEY HAVE CLOSED THEIR EYES, OTHERWISE THEY WOULD SEE WITH THEIR EYES, HEAR WITH THEIR EARS, AND UNDERSTAND WITH THEIR HEART AND RETURN, AND I WOULD HEAL THEM.'

But blessed are your eyes, because they see; and your ears, because they hear. For truly I say to you that many prophets and righteous men desired to see what you see, and did not see it, and to hear what you hear, and did not hear it.

Hear then the parable of the sower. When anyone hears the word of the kingdom and does not understand it, the evil one comes and snatches away what has been sown in his heart. This is the one on whom seed was sown beside the road. The one on whom seed was sown on the rocky places, this is the man who hears the word and immediately receives it with joy; yet he has no firm root in himself, but is only temporary, and when affliction or persecution arises because of the word, immediately he falls away. And the one on whom seed was sown among the thorns, this is the man who hears the word, and the worry of the world and the deceitfulness of wealth choke the word, and it becomes unfruitful. And the one on whom seed was sown on the good soil, this is the man who hears the word and understands it; who indeed bears fruit and brings forth, some a hundredfold, some sixty, and some thirty."

In this parable, Jesus speaks of four different levels of soil. He likens each level of soil to a condition of a person's soul. As you read, consider and remember the four levels of communication, and the four levels of relationship.

1. Trampled, hardened – describing the soul of a person who does not understand Kingdom life, and who dismisses the Word as not being necessary for living.

2. Rocky, shallow – describing the soul of a person who has many hard and stony places in their heart. They can hear the Truth and have a desire to learn, until they are corrected or confronted. They lack the ability to follow through, and things outside the Presence of God gain attention and loyalty.

3. Weedy, thorny – describing the soul of a person who has battles with distraction in their desire to walk a solid walk with Jesus.

4. Good soil – 30, 60 and 100 fold – describing the soul of a person who receives the seed of God's Truth with an open heart and responds with obedience and teach-ability. Notice that good soil has degrees of fruitfulness.

In this parable, Jesus refers to these differing qualities of soil as being descriptive of the state of the heart of man. This was the first parable Jesus told in His ministry on earth; which makes it highly significant in looking at how God views the condition of our soul when it comes to our ability to relate to Him and to Truth. For me personally, it reminds me that Abba Father made man and woman in His image, placing them in the Garden of Eden to cultivate it and keep it. That would mean that our God has always been a cultivator; a Gardener of the soul, if you will.

What is most encouraging about this parable is that soil quality can be changed. Just like a physical garden, hard work is involved to break up the hard soil, remove the stones, and weeds. And, just like a physical garden, fertilizer is added to soften and enrich the soil. In relational terms, the "fertilizer" which enriches the soil of the heart of man, would be the life lessons (God-given) we take away from the painful experiences in our lives.

As we walk through the first five books in the primer series, please remember the levels of soil, and how they relate to the levels of communication and relationships. Over the past twenty years, I have used these comparisons in the ministry of pastoral counseling; seeing results in the lives of believers as well as disciples.

The four types of soil Jesus referred to in the Sower's parable, directly relate to the four levels of communication and relationship, listed and shown below.

IQ	**1. Cliches** **2. Facts**	*Image based – intelligence* *Task and Doing oriented*
EQ	**3. Values, Principles (male)** **Morals, Feelings (female)** **4. Yearnings and Needs**	*Truth based – heart of man* *Relationship and Be-ing oriented*
Core	**Inner Child**	*Real self/spiritual perceptions* *Obedience and Inner Approval oriented*

There are many areas of relational living which correspond to these four levels of relationship. For a more detailed addressing of this subject, and to pinpoint a person's placement in growth, please consider utilizing the G.E.M.S. Personal Assessment Tool, (Section M), by Debbye Graafsma. *(Available through Awakened to Grow, or online.)*

When a person lives in a healthy state, individual Personhood is expressed through the whole being. This is called Congruency. On a practical level, the person portrays the same personality in all settings of living. They are strong enough in their Core to withstand the pressures and intimidations of varying environments.

When we come to Christ, becoming believers for the first time, very rarely is anyone congruent. That process begins when we choose to yield to the Spirit of God, allowing Him access and permission to shape us into the likeness of Christ.

In considering these truths, I have provided a chart on the next page, which combines the work of cultivation or gardening, with the condition of the soil on each level. It is my hope it will encourage you as you encounter believers as well as disciples in your ministry as a helper/counselor.

The Sower and the Seed: Becoming A Cultivated & Well Watered Garden

"The Lord will guide you continually, and satisfy your soul in drought, and strengthen your bones; and you shall be like a watered garden, and like a spring of water, whose waters do not fail." Isaiah 58:11

The Parable: Matthew 13:3-9 and 18-23

Type of Soil Vs 3-9	Jesus' Meaning vs 18-23	Condition of the Heart	A Gardener's Solution	Spiritual Application
1. Seed on the wayside -- was devoured by birds	Not understood Devil steals it Survivor mentality	Numb, Trodden down By reason of conditioning has become rock hard feels used.	Soak with water. Break up crusty earth. Dig deep earth. Dig. Remove rocks. Add fertilizer and conditioners before planting. Feed well.	Has learned to believe a lie Life experiences have wounded and closed the heart. (emotionally and spiritually)
2. Seed on stony places -- no depth, withered by elements	Receives, but has No depth in himself to make application, is offended by difficulty and falls away only. No joy. "Tell me what the rules are – I'll do that."	Unaware of deeper possibilities. Too many hard things with no understanding or ability to resolve. Functioning plants well.	Water well to loosen earth. Remove stones. Dig down to rock. Add fertilizer and conditioners. Feed	Sees the stones. Feel stuck. Difficulties argue with the love of God. The heart wants to trust, but fears repetition of pain. (trusts self most)
3. Seed among thorns -- new growth crowded by weeds	Receives, but has so many other things "going on right now" any application is squeezed out, becomes unfruitful	Aware of deeper growth Drawn by Holy Spirit – is easily distracted by obligations and responsibilities. Content to maintain on surface but lives unfulfilled	Weed out crowded growth beds. Spade around plants for aerating soil. Add fertilizer. Condition soil. Water well. Monitor for sprouts of weed seeds not pulled on first try.	Is weed aware, assumes they are normal – is used to emotional clutter. Fearful of Change – task oriented for security. (works based. Condemnation focused, fear driven)
4. Seed on good ground -- yielded a crop	Receives, understands, allows it to grow, and bears life-fruit	Open and vulnerable Teachable, receiving truth and making application personal changes daily indicate growth	Maintain weed free status. Maintain condition of soil. Regular cultivation and aeration for health. New plantings and pruning as applicable.	Maturity takes time, growth takes time. There are no substitutes. Discipleship involves discovery. Emotional health and spiritual maturity cannot be separated. Daily maintenance will ensure continued development.

Section Two
Facts about Anger

"What Does Anger Look Like?"

Within our world, and especially within the church, we as people of God, are barraged with conflicting ideas about anger.

Is anger wrong? Is it a sin to be angry? When is anger appropriate? Is it possible to be a solid and growing disciple of Jesus Christ and experience anger?

This year in the United States:

2 million American women will be severely beaten by their husbands.
Thousands of husbands will be battered by their angry wives.
1.5 million children will be abused by their parents.
Thousands of elderly parents will be abused by their adult children.

Family violence is the most common crime in our nation

Last year: There was a violent crime – every 11 seconds.
There was a murder --- Every 16 minutes
There was a robbery –Every 50 seconds
There was an aggravated assault --Every 40 seconds
In the case of a murder – the victim knew their killer well, more than 50% of the time.
In those cases, an angry argument had preceded the murder *every time.*

Currently: Every five minutes, a woman is raped in the United States.
Every fifteen seconds, a woman is beaten.

Three of four women will be victims of at least one violent crime during their lifetime.
Although 4 million women are battered, only 1.5 million seek medical assistance for injuries by battering each year.

The statistics indicate the majority (more than 65%) of violent crimes are against women.

What does that say about our ability to handle conflict as a nation?

Last year: There were 84,000 forcible rapes.

This per capita rate is: 13x higher than Great Britain
4x higher than Germany
20+x higher than Japan

In *all* of these instances, Anger was blamed as the issue responsible for the crime. However, it was not the Anger itself that was to blame. *IT WAS THE CHOSEN EXPRESSION OF THAT ANGER…*

For Anger to be handled properly it must be managed properly.

Sadly, it is only the minority of us who are able to manage our anger, or express it properly. And, sadly, the statistics among church-going people are not very different than non-church attenders.

The fact is: We all have anger issues.

Here are four different mismanagements angry people often utilize:

1. **Internalizing** – *Often, we are completely unaware we are angry, until a physical symptom materializes in our physical body, due to unresolved anger and pain. In this type of anger, the person has a difficult time even admitting they are angry. Instead, they just continue living in with a constant low level of inner stress and irritation. This person many times will deal with a pervasive illness, or series of illnesses, and adopt a sense of victimization.*

2. **Exploding** – *This person seems to live with a lit fuse most of the time. Those around them are never sure what will cause the "bomb" to explode or when it will explode. As a result, those in their sphere of influence live in a sense of constant apprehension. Many times, this person will wonder why no one wants to be close to them, or spend time in deep discussion, considering they are misunderstood, and are "just completely honest and direct."*

3. **Inwardly Driving and punishing** – *This person has learned to survive in a probably angry environment by absorbing blame, many times allowing themselves to become guilt-motivated. This person has learned to hate himself or herself, because they have come to believe they "always" cause anger in others. As a result, they avoid conflict, and angry situations. They are many times depressed and unable to cope with the emotions of others around them.*

4. **Denying and Minimalizing** – *This person believes anger is unacceptable as an emotion, but the anger cannot be hidden. As a result, the anger they feel is usually hidden. It is possible the person conducts life in a passive aggressive manner, hiding the anger behind something else, such as sarcastic wit or criticisms. This person avoids confronting the issues they feel, but re-directs attention to tasks rather than developing health in their relationships.*

The Word of God gives us solutions for these questions, and they don't involve just shutting down.

Did you know? There are root causes for anger.

Anger is a God-provided emotion, designed for a constructive purpose.

"What Is the Proper Purpose for Anger?"

1. **The capacity for Anger is biological. It is part of our God-provided design, and is as natural as breathing.**

    When anger is aroused, our bodies release adrenaline. This causes us to be alert and aware. This is a survival mechanism. When we feel endangered, or wounded in some way, anger is the sense of mobilization and empowerment we suddenly feel to take action. What we do with that sense of empowerment is an action which studies show is learned and then chosen habitually. When our chosen method of handling anger is damaging to self and others, it must be addressed and changed for us to develop healthy patterns of living.

2. **How we express our Anger is learned, rather than genetically inherited. Therefore, it can be un-learned.**

3. **Anger is the sense of empowerment. In itself, it is not Aggression, or even Assertiveness. Those actions are chosen in response to the sense of inward emotion.**

    More than 85% of angry expressions are filled with negative approaches and unkind attitudes. This is why we many times misunderstand the purpose of Anger in our lives as human beings.
    There is a way to be angry and still treat others positively, working for a goal to benefit the common good, without attack or aggressiveness. It is possible to be angry and remain positive, yet assertive. Such a situation will require clear thinking, and the ability to express true feelings and needs. This approach prevents damage being done in relationships, and can actually work to draw people in conflict closer together in relationship.

4. **Actions should not be taken impulsively when a person is Angry.**

    It is almost inevitable that damage in relationships will happen when actions, or re-actions, happen impulsively in Anger. Many times, such impulses manifest as the person's desire to steer the outcome of a situation *outside* of their control; the results of which are damaging and hard to repair.

5. The healthy way to deal with Anger is to utilize it for a constructive purpose.

The organization, "Mothers Against Drunk Drivers," (MADD) was founded by a hurt and angry mother. Such an action is a constructive use of Anger as an emotion. In order to see our Anger as a positive emotion, however, it is necessary to accept responsibility for what we feel in the first place, and then be willing to take steps to heal. Current research indicates that the negative expression of Anger does not cause that Anger to dissipate. Rather, it is a catalyst for more anger and subsequent justification of aggressive behavior. We see the results of that misunderstanding as to the expression of our anger every day in the culture we live in. Additionally, further studies indicate that the witnessing of violence and anger; whether in the home, in the culture, or through media expressions, actually teaches, models and imprints those behaviors on the mind, causing a multiplication of those behaviors in the culture.

> *"The greatest remedy for Anger is delay."*
>
> ■ *Thomas Paine*

"What Anger is NOT…."

It is not unfriendliness.
It is not a sense of hostility.
It is not hatred.
It is not a negative attitude.
It is not fear.
It is not judgmentalism.
It is not violent.
It is not withdrawal.
It is not punishing.
It is not unkindness.
It is not depression.
It is not rudeness.
It is not a hardness of heart.
It is not legalism.
It is not cold aloofness.
It is not silence.

"What Anger IS….."

Anger is a like a car started and sitting in the driveway, waiting for the driver to choose the direction, speed and gear for travel.

Anger is the result of our hurt, or fear. It is the awareness of the injustice we have been exposed to. (When we give in to resentment, we develop a negative attitude towards living. This unprocessed resentment can build over time, and harden into cynicism and pessimism. This end result is what we recognize as hostility. Left untreated, hostility develops into hatred.)

Anger is neither positive nor negative. It requires healthy management.

Anger is given to help us develop skills to be able to cope effectively.

Anger is provided to help bring our inner pain to an absolute minimum, preserving our understanding of our personal value, our needs and our convictions.

Anger is designed to be a good thing. When we give in to embarrassment or shame because we are angry, we stop the growth process.

The Principles of Change

1. There is always hope for change.

2. We cannot change what we do not acknowledge.

3. The primary ingredient of the change process is Truth (in love) in an open heart.

4. We cannot change others. We can only change ourselves.

5. Repentance is the only catalyst (beginning place) for change to occur.

6. Our inner brokenness is the beginning place for repentance, and therefore Change.

7. Changes we seek to make within ourselves without the help of the Holy Spirit, will never be permanent, because they are based in our own works and effort.

8. We cannot expect God to give grace or healing, when we are unwilling to repent.

9. Growth cannot happen without change.

10. Change will involve both forward and backward motion, always with our eyes fixed upon the goal of becoming like Christ.

11. The Doorway into the Change Process is guarded from the inside, by a person who must open the door from the inside. It cannot be forced open.

12. Change must be chosen, sometimes with struggle.

13. Change comes as a result of Training, not as a result of simply trying, using the same tools we have used in the past.

14. Change is a process. It takes time. What took years to tear down will require a season of hard work to redeem, repair and restore.

15. It takes intentional maintenance for change to remain.

Copyright 2005, dg atg

> *When is the last time you got angry at someone treating you with respect?"*
>
> *— Joseph Shrand MD*

Section Three.
The Sources of Anger

Did you know?

Anger is <u>not</u> a primary emotion.

Rather, …..

1. Anger is realized as an almost automatic inner response to the circumstances around us.

2. Anger is also part of the Grief Cycle. (Many times, when a client of mine discovers this, they can trace the beginning of their Anger Management issues to a single traumatic event, that has been waiting, unprocessed, for healing.)

3. Hurtful Anger is a learned behavior – We see it modeled by our authority figures, and peers. Then, because we see another person get what they want because they are angry, we mistakenly assume becoming angry will give us the same results. Sometimes, becoming forceful and expressing bad behaviors might give us immediate results of control, but those results never last for long; they must be continually reinforced with more and more Anger.

Anger's Path

Life Approach Attitude (model/imprinting)	The Message Believed (about self) (activator/trigger)	First Emotion (below the surface)	Secondary Emotion (evident behavior)
Everyone should just be nice and get along.	People should listen when I tell them how to get along.	Hurt; Fear of Rejection Fear of Conflict	ANGER
My life should be easier than it is.	Life should be fair; Others should take care of me.	Exclusion; Justice Frustration; Insecurity	ANGER
I need everyone to respect/like me.	There is something wrong with me.	Rejection: Disapproval Shame; Confusion	ANGER
I should be in control of what happens in my life.	Other people should allow me to have the control.	Fear of Vulnerability Fear of Rejection	ANGER
I should always know what to do when bad things happen in my life.	I don't know what to do in this situation. I am relationally un-tooled.	Embarrassment Fear of Rejection Fear of Being Known	ANGER
I should always be "on top" of things	I can't meet the expectations I have/others have.	Shame; Helplessness Self-Hatred	ANGER
Mistakes/Failings are unacceptable.	If I fail, or am wrong, I am unacceptable.	Fear of Disapproval Abandonment; Self-Hatred	ANGER
I should use my skills, and not do things I feel are beneath me.	Others should do the things I don't want to do for me.	Entitlement Improper Self-Image	ANGER
I should never make mistakes.	I cannot be wrong, or apologize/admit weakness.	Pride; Entitlement; Confusion Shame; Fear of Vulnerability	ANGER
I have to earn my way.	My value is determined by what I know how to do.	Overwhelmed; Fear of Rejection; Self-rejection; Guilt; Futility	ANGER

CONFLICT OCCURS (between columns 2 and 3)

©2010 dg/atg

Considering Anger's Path

When we allow our emotions to choose unkind behaviors and words after we have experienced frustration, fear, or wounded-ness, we actually end up revealing embarrassing and vulnerable areas to those we injure. And believe it or not, Anger is actually an expression of weakness, rather than of strength or power.

When my husband and I were first married, he would take on construction jobs in order to help with our income. We were both college students, and expenses were…. Well, you know. I remember going with him to a job on a particular occasion. He was helping a homeowner repair wiring in their dining room. At one point, none of us had realized the power had not been turned off. I don't remember much about the circumstance, except the image of Bill holding two shielded pieces of wire (which we thought were devoid of electricity). Suddenly, without warning, between the two ends of wire, a bright blue arc exploded, bringing connection where none had existed before. Needless to say, the homeowner ran to the breaker box, quickly shutting off the power.

The negative behaviors associated with Anger's Path usually work the same way. Whenever there is a gap in our personal emotional congruency, we will find ourselves at a loss to know how to respond in certain situations. When we feel the primary emotions charted on the prior page, we run to the emotional "toolbox" we have been adding "tools" to since our childhood. When we discover, sometimes without being cognitively aware, that we have no ability to deal with the situation or relationship at hand, we "arc." We cover the distance of the unknown and unequipped area in order to protect ourselves. After all, shouldn't we already have the tools we need to "fix" the situation?

When we choose to "arc out," most of the time, our expressions are inappropriate and damaging. We end up hindering, or even destroying the relationships we have worked so hard to build. Then, later, when we are once more dwelling in a rational mindset, we find we have deepened to an even greater degree the sense of powerlessness we already feel.

It is possible, with a willingness to do the hard work involved, to bring the sense of Anger into alignment with Abba Father's created design. This means disciplining our rationality to stay vigilant and in charge of our reactions and responses. Without rational personal governing, led by the Holy Spirit of God, we will continue to live our lives in condemnation, shame and frustration.

The point is, Anger left to itself is destructive. Harnessed, it becomes an arsenal of power for growth, change and development.

Did you know Unprocessed Anger will affect your physical health?

Researchers now agree, as the commonality of materials show the following: Negative Emotions actually create disease. In fact, the CDC (Center for Disease Control and Prevention) recently stated that 85% of all diseases have a strong link to your emotional state.

Secondly, the expenditure of energy in negative Anger experiences is now proven to cause weakening of the immune system. When Anger begins to call the shots, your body readies itself to respond to a perceived threat. Normal body processes halt... and many brain centers begin firing in way which alter brain chemistry.

Thirdly, those who explode in Angry expressions are significantly more likely to have arterial calcium deposits occur – This is a primary indicator of heart attack risk.

And lastly, the practice of "stuffing it" isn't good for your body either. Studies have found that repressing Anger is worse for your body than actually lashing out.

So, what should an angry person do?

This is why God created the Body of Christ – It is His Plan; designed to provide us with safe people, and a community where healing and growth can take place, without fear of rejection, disapproval or reprisals.

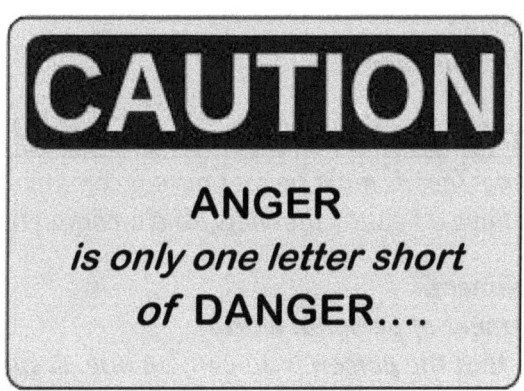

"If I pretend I have no anger and try to bury it, it will bury me--- literally, by triggering a heart attack, a stroke, digestive problems, migraines, stress in my back and neck, or stress based diseases."

"If I let anger out in the wrong way, it can ruin my marriage, alienate my children, and get me fired from my job."

"If I somehow turn it around on myself, it can tear my personal sense of value apart, destroy my motivation and initiative, and set me up for all kinds of physical and emotional pain and torment."

"If I fail to process it when I experience it, it may turn into resentment and bitterness. If it does, I can become hostile, negative and impossible to be around. I will certainly stop having any expectations for life to improve."

Some people deal with anger when personal needs are not met......

Physical Needs for Wilderness Survival
(in order of significance and importance)

1. Air
2. Sleep
3. Shelter/warmth (body protected from the weather)
4. Water
5. Food
6. A Positive Attitude
7. Medical Attention
8. Sanitation
9. Innovation and Invention
10. Navigation
11. Community
12. Comfort
13. Emotional Well Being
14. Recognition and/or Success

Emotional Core Needs (Environment/Atmospheric)

These core yearnings/needs must be met during cognitive (physical) development, for a person to have a healthy life-view, and a complete sense of Personhood.

1. A safe secure environment.
2. A constant reinforcement of personal worth
3. Repeated messages that the person is valued, unique, & special
4. Unconditional Love & acceptance
5. Basic Care & nurturing
6. Encouragement to Grow – develop personal gifts & talents.
7. A pathway to fellowship with God
8. Connection & belonging
9. Feeling needed & Useful
10. Inner emotional & character building for destiny fulfillment

When our physical needs are met, we begin to focus on emotional needs. Undue focusing on emotional needs will create a cycle of self-focus, destroying utility in the life, creating a demanding and anger based existence.
Learn to recognize essential from non-essential needs.
How important to you are the needs of others?

Where does the awareness of unmet needs affect us? (We are all unique. However, most unmet needs affect the core of our being, and therefore touch all aspect of our Personhood.)

Levels of Communication

1. Clichés
2. Facts

IQ — Outer Life

Task & Doing

IMAGE BASED

Tangible

Wall of self protection—pride+fear=control

IMPACT POINT of Unmet needs

Inner Life

Intangible

3. Principles/Values/Morals/Feelings
4. Yearnings/Needs

EQ

Relationship & Being

TRUTH BASED

Line of selfless choice

5. Deep sense of security & approval

OBEDIENCE BASED

IQ & EQ

Core Person (Inner Child)

© dg atg

Because Anger is designed to serve us in its positive form, as a type of empowerment, we can mistakenly utilize it as a substitute for an under-developed or missing element of Personhood. Additionally, Anger is many times misunderstood as an expression of strength and/or manhood in many circles.

What is Personhood?

In order for a person to develop and grow in a healthy manner, there are four elements of personhood which optimally should be provided and communicated during a child's "in the nest" years of development. As an illustration of this principle, I use a barstool to show the need for uniform and equal provision of each element. When any leg of the "stool" is missing, or allowed to be "too short, or uneven," in the life, a child will grow up with specific gaps in their awareness of what healthy Personhood looks like.

They will find it difficult to interact and maintain long-term relationships with others.

Elements of Personhood:

1. Community – the sense that I am part of a larger picture than myself; that I fit within that group

2. Relationship – specific and intentional emotional attachments within community in which I am mutually committed to growth and connection on an ongoing basis.

3. Empowerment – the confidence drawn from healthy bonds of relationship, enabling the ability to express inner and outer life processes: the power to live an honest portrayal of inner motivations.

4. Voice – any expression of the inner self. Examples include: speaking, singing, musical and/or creative expressions, dance, art, any form of clearly communicating what is inwardly believed and felt.

Voice and Empowerment   couple together
Community and Relationship   couple together.

a. When voice is suppressed, empowerment is also suppressed.
b. Voice will back-build until a trigger occurs in the life, and then *anger* will act as an empowering mechanism.
c. Depending upon the amount of improper perceptions active in the life, a person will act or react with rage, or another unhealthy expression of anger.
d. In this instance, Anger serves as a catalyst for voice to be expressed.

Anger is also one of the steps of Grief, designed to help us deal with our personal losses by providing us with a sense of empowerment to walk forward from our losses with positive change.

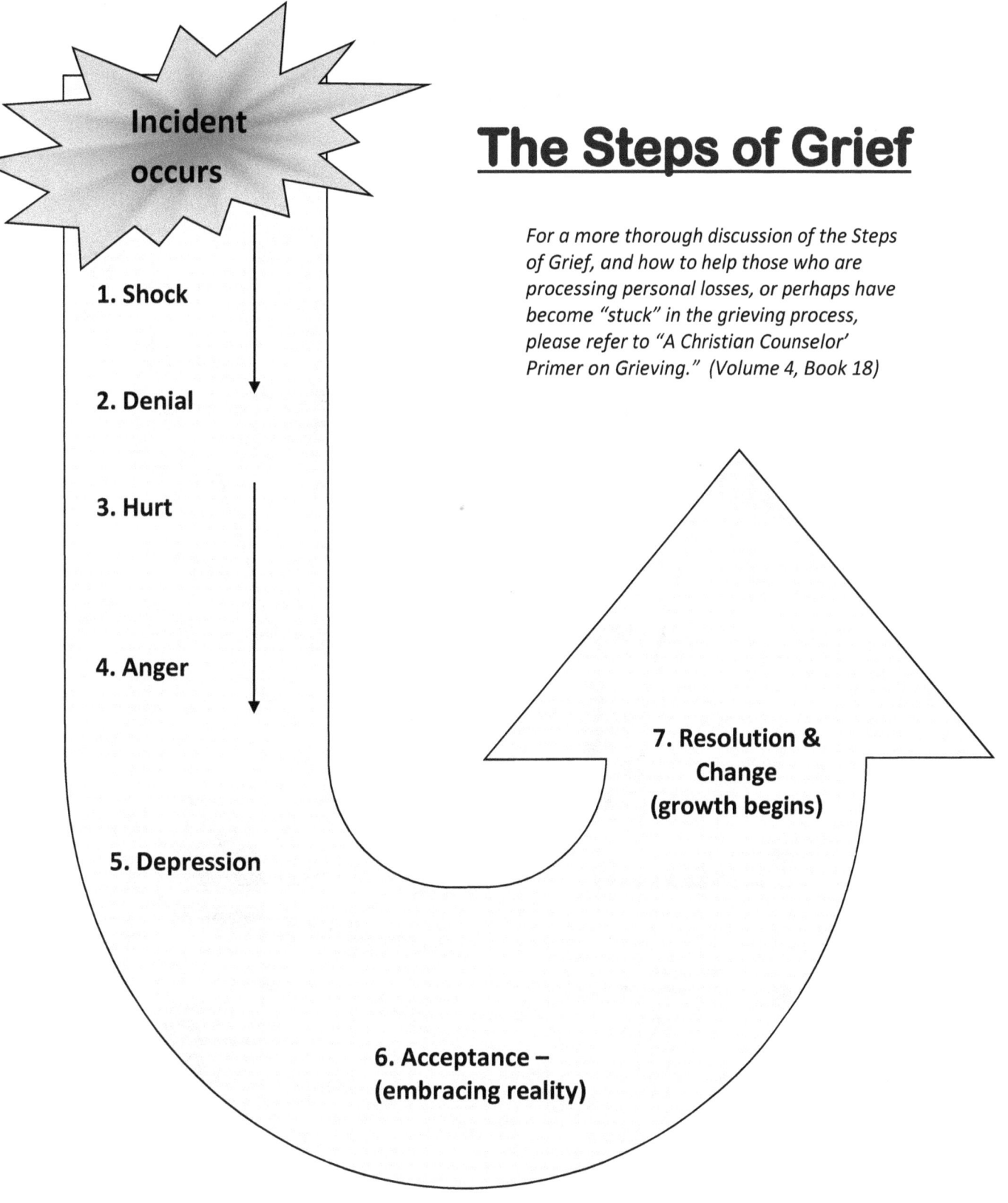

The Steps of Grief

For a more thorough discussion of the Steps of Grief, and how to help those who are processing personal losses, or perhaps have become "stuck" in the grieving process, please refer to "A Christian Counselor' Primer on Grieving." (Volume 4, Book 18)

Incident occurs

1. Shock
2. Denial
3. Hurt
4. Anger
5. Depression
6. Acceptance – (embracing reality)
7. Resolution & Change (growth begins)

When a person, for one reason or another, becomes stalled in the processing of his or her losses, the Steps of Grief also stall. The person begins to cycle, many times "bouncing" off the "unacceptable" form of grief. Here is my understanding of what that will look like in a person's life on a practical level.

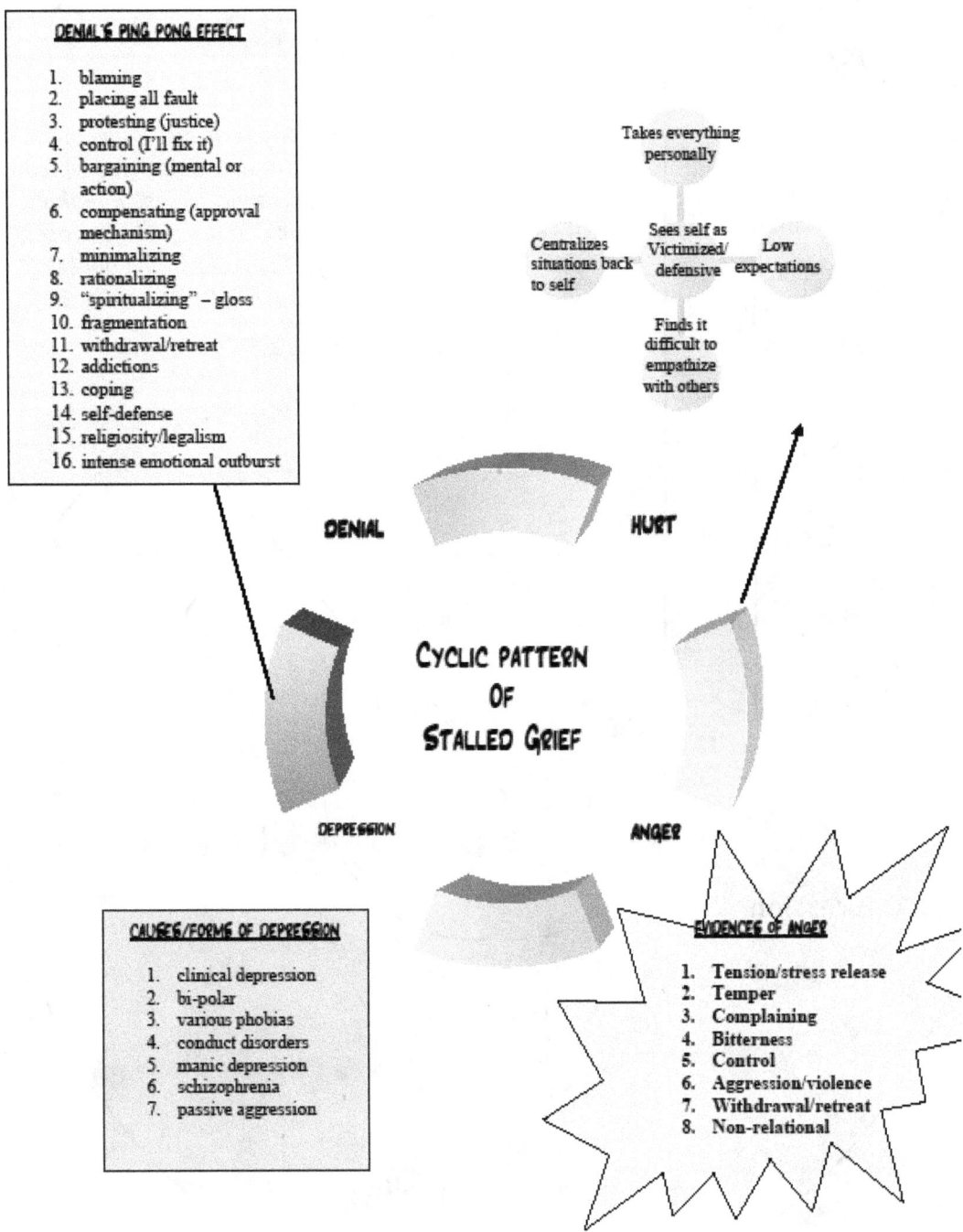

"Dangerous Thinking About Anger....."

1. ***"I have to be allowed to blow up when I'm angry. I'm not responsible for what I say when I'm angry. Everyone should know I don't mean it."*** The thinking that anger is un-harness-able, and must be unleashed for a person to experience relief from it.

> **The truth is.... We are each responsible for our behaviors, and for our responses to the situations that trigger those behaviors.**

2. ***"Just be glad I didn't hit you! I have to get this out!"*** The thinking that I need to say the words that come into my head when I'm angry, and follow through with those actions impulsively.

> **The truth is.... Angry words draw the same responses as physical violence. We lose relationships. Many times we are angry because we have wrongly believed that all of our unmet needs should be met. It is unreasonable to expect other people to meet our unmet needs. We are each responsible for our behaviors, and for our responses to the situations that trigger those behaviors.**

3. ***"It's always wrong to get angry. I don't let that happen."*** This view says it is honest behavior to deny feelings of hurt and resentment. Sometimes this is a trained behavior, and the feeling centers of the person become anesthetized. We become detached, and unprocessed anger is internalized on the physical being.

> **The truth is.... When we deny our feelings, we become factual, unfeeling and alone. Those in relationship with this person many times feel critiqued and judged. People who refuse to deal with anger in this manner, also show physical symptoms of illness.**

4. *"I shouldn't get angry. I should expect more from myself."* This approach teaches me to hate myself and I punish myself for feeling angry.

>**The truth is…. Many people who punish themselves in this way deal with long term depression, and may even commit suicide.**

5. *"I'm not angry, I'm just tired of being surrounded by idiots."* This kind of thinking indicates the mindset of a passive-aggressive person; someone who is angry, and attacks in an underhanded, or hidden method.

>**The truth is…. This person does not take initiative in relationships, and does not assert themselves into relationships. They wait for their personal needs to be met, and if they are unmet, the person indicates they have been let down in some way. This person usually denies they are angry, but it is more than evident to everyone else in their life that Anger is their life motivation.**

Note: These persons are passive-aggressive in their approach to Anger. They are known to be charmers. If a person gets lured in to a relationship with them, from that point onward, they should be prepared to always carry the ball, never to score, and to end up behind by at least 100 points.

If you compare this anger management system with the exploder, you might decide that it would be better to live with an exploder – at least they get it over with. With a passive-aggressive person,

>If you confront him – he slips away
>If you walk away – he says you're not trying
>If you give your best – it's not good enough

What is healthy, is to look the passive-aggressive person in the eye, and tell them you are struggling with anger. Ask them to look you in the eye and discuss it; working together for a constructive change. People with passive anger never look you in the eye – they just try to get even.

Many people who deal with passive anger are pouters. When things don't go their way, they become sullen. They remove their person from you, without ever moving away. They distance themselves, creating guilt. This causes us to ask, "Are you okay? Is something wrong?" A healthy, normal person might tell you that they are dealing with a reason they can't get hold of, and that they are sad, or that they are just worn out from a strenuous week. Not a pouter. The response will be selfish and immature. And it will never have a positive consequence.

The most dangerous passively angry person is the one who uses sarcastic wit to stay in control of a situation or a relationship. This is known as verbal aggression, and, even if it is aimed at oneself, it is a jab, and is designed to penetrate. It's funny, so you laugh, but when the laughter dies away, steel points are visible, and the damage is done.

Sarcastic people are usually intensely concerned about how they compare with others, and they do not take other people's feelings very seriously. They are hard to confront, because their say, "Sorry, I was just being funny." And the person walks away thinking that they must be crazy in some way, or over sensitive. These people are dart throwers, and even though they are funny, after a while, they find themselves without any close friends to truly connect with.

It is never a positive choice to choose a short-term and temporary victory, by causing emotional damage, and a long-term loss of relationship.

> "Never respond to an angry person with a fiery comeback, even if he deserves it...Don't allow his anger to become your anger."
>
> — Bohdi Sanders

Conflict Resolution is one of the primary foundation stones for any healthy relationship.

Unresolved conflict distills into Anger, eventually forming into Distance.

Section Four.
The Counselor's Role in Helping Those Who Struggle with Anger

Most people who struggle with Anger issues are unaware they are damaging the relationships around them. In fact, without exception, every person I have had the privilege to help through their Anger issues has initially felt misunderstood and attacked by the assessments of others regarding their Anger. When I have counseled with those seeking Anger Management skills, the initial issue requiring attention in the client's life was Defensiveness.

It is important for the counselor to remember that Anger is a secondary emotion. In the process of helping an angry individual, you will discover the wounds being protected by the Anger. In my own experience: the deeper the wound, the more fierce the anger.

After Defense Mechanisms are addressed and dismantled, the person with Anger issues needs to come to a place of desiring to be changed more than they desire comfort. In saying that, let me make a few suggestions:

a. Never allow yourself to take a client's issues personally.
b. Never become reactive with a client; anger is contagious – don't "catch" it.
c. Always listen very carefully to the words the client says. Over the years, I have discovered that people usually mean exactly what they say.
d. Give your client time to process what they are learning. Most people who deal with Anger issues, do so because they have been the victims of large quantities of impatience and anger themselves. You may have to explain and re-explain information several times before they really grasp it.

"A gentle answer turns away wrath,
but a harsh word stirs up anger." Proverbs 15:1

"When the anger is intense,

the person with Asperger's syndrome

may be in a 'blind rage' and unable

to see the signals indicating

that it would be appropriate to stop.

Feelings of anger can also be

in response in situations where

we would expect other emotions.

I have noted that sadness

may be expressed as anger."

— Tony Attwood

Here are a few materials to help you in the process of helping others:

Most behaviors which people come into a counselor's office regarding will be cyclical in nature. Anger issues, as well as addictions, are cyclical in nature. Additionally, differing types of Anger will cause differing cycles of emotion.

The experience of a person who battles with explosive or more expressive Anger will look like this:

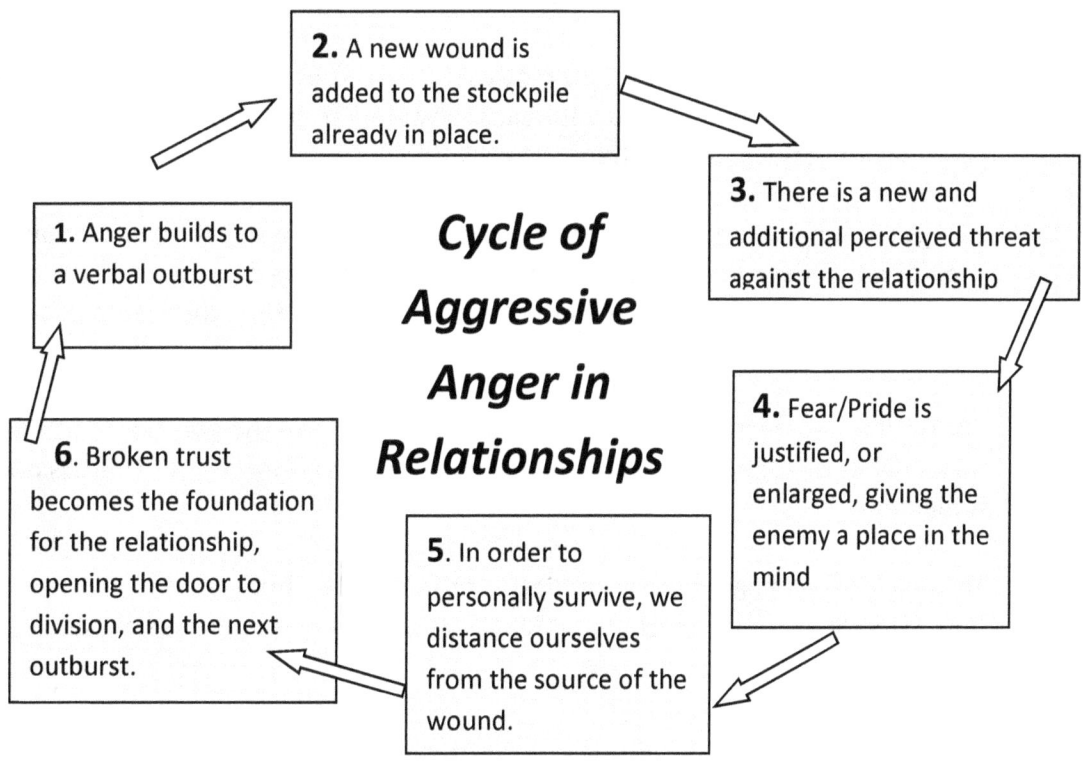

Discoveries Required for Healing People with Exploding/Aggressive Anger Expressions:

1. Yelling and screaming are forms of verbal abuse. We wound others when we overpower them to gain control.

2. When we explode, we don't get what we really want. We only get what we ask for in the immediate realm. What we really want is a sense of connection and mutual acceptance.

3. Yelling might cause immediate change, but we lose respect and relationship.

4. Telling family member what we really think might clear our heads, but after a while those family members avoid us; and find other ways to spend time instead of relating.

5. Threatening our employees might motivate them – but we lose continuity. We keep having to train a new one, and with each new worker, it becomes harder to establish a positive professional atmosphere. Morale is low.

6. Being strict might keep our children in line, but no communication is ever pursued from their point of view. We find ourselves completely removed from being personally involved in their lives; much less how they feel, or what they think about their lives. They begin to avoid us.

7. Controlling circumstances might make a spouse respond the way we want them to, but no romance or spontaneous joy and fun exists in the relationship. There is no sense of fulfillment.

8. Throwing things might help us do better or feel better, but we don't receive understanding as a result of our actions. We usually find ourselves alone.

Something to consider:

80% of couples who enter into verbal abuse, end up in physical combat.

Most couples who enter into verbal abuse, experience runaway children, separation and divorce, terminations of relationships; explosive anger changes things – they are never the same...

We Sometimes Think that Anger will help us to protect ourselves....

Angry expression is <u>not</u> limited to open aggression. Many times, we think we need to become angry in order to protect our personal worth, needs, or convictions at someone else's expense. Negative and aggressive angry expressions also include explosiveness, rage, intimidation, and blame. It also includes bickering, criticism, griping, complaining, and sarcasm.

This type of angry expression indicates a powerful insensitivity to the needs of others, as well as a probably tendency towards narcissism.

Sometimes, we suffer from the misconception of needing to portray and Perfect Image. For some reason, usually stemming from our Family of Origin, we are intimidated with a perceived threat of rejection or disapproval if we sense others think we are less than perfect. Any indication that we might be at fault, or not be informed, "lights the fuse," and our anger is aroused.

Sadly, our need for approval becomes a driving force. It is our goal. Anything that might indicate we carry a flaw: criticism, suggestions, correction, or instruction trigger an offense. We then allow our emotions to tell us to "wall" off. So, we reject those who criticize or correct, or might seek to instruct us.

We become unable to receive from anyone who could help us.

This is Pride in its worst form.

Internalized, or "Stuffed" Anger

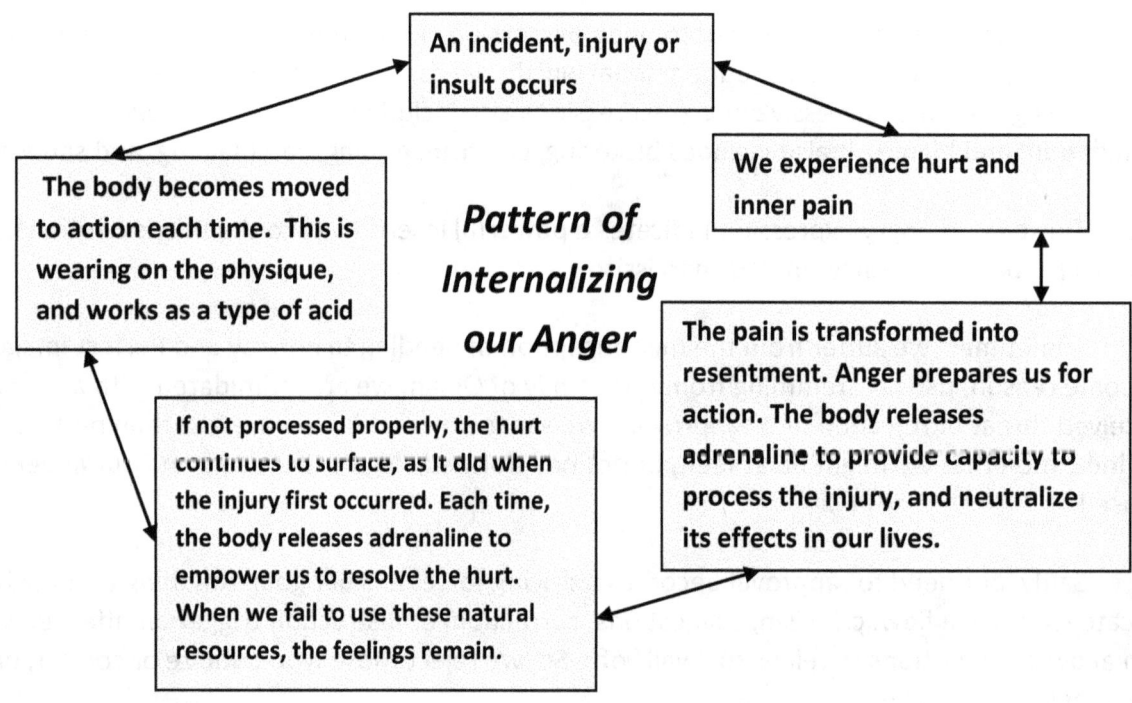

A note about the human body's Sympathetic Nervous system –

Our Creator has placed crisis response systems within the human body. In an experienced emergency, these systems prepare us to deal with unforeseen and immediate concerns. The heart beats faster, our adrenal glands secrete adrenalin, our liver releases sugar into the body, our muscles tense and our arteries constrict. These mechanisms allow us to respond to situations we consider threatening, both internal and external.

This response is many times mislabeled "anger."

Studies show that as children, many people learn to become sick in order to avoid expressions of anger. For example, if parents who are usually unkind and dominating become kind and attentive when a child is ill, that child learns to become sick to experience an expression of love. Many times even into adulthood, this learned behavior is repeated, and continued. Experience has taught this person to handle their anger in this manner.

The purpose of anger is to give us the wherewithal to manage our environment – particularly those parts which cause us to feel hurt, frustrated or fearful.. If we manage that environment poorly, we experience a sense of inadequacy and helplessness. The problems seem too difficult to solve.

When we discover ourselves to be inadequate, we then focus upon our inability, and particularly our failings. Our society reinforces the emphasizing of defects. So, our sense of personal value is reduced to a dangerously low level. We assess ourselves on the basis of what we have failed to accomplish, rather than seeing realistic appreciation for those things that have been accomplished.

We say things like this on the inside:

> "I should have gotten more done today."
> "I haven't done a very good job keeping my car clean."
> "I'm a failure as a person. I really should be more involved at church."
> "I ought to be able to make a basket every time when I play basketball."
> "I didn't get the bills paid."

A person who struggles with Anger issues, many times sets unrealistic goals for him or herself. Additionally, they only can see those areas where life is going wrong. They see what is missing, instead of focusing on what is going right. This perspective brings a negative life outlook, with no expectations for positive occurrences.

Helplessness and the sense of powerlessness that fuels Anger can cause a person to feel trapped. Once that occurs, depression also becomes a part of daily existence.

One of the main reasons a person becomes angry is the emotion of feeling de-valued or invalidated. When past experiences have left us feeling unworthy, or insignificant, we will tend to be more sensitive to feelings of being devalued. Also, if our needs were the center of our world as children, it will create in us the sense of having to have all of our needs met continually as adults in order to be happy or secure. If this is our experience, we will make those demands of others in our lives, in order to reinforce and maintain the feeling of being the center of everyone's world.

Anger is designed by Abba Father to be constructive, allowing us to discover new areas of life, and grow, despite our emotional and intellectual pain.

> *"When I am angry, I can write, pray, and preach well, for then my whole temperament is quickened, my understanding sharpened, and all mundane vexations and temptations are gone."*   Martin Luther

Individuals who "stuff" or internalize their Anger, usually live with a low level of inner conflict. Because the Anger has been turned inward, onto their own person, this person will mis-label Anger, as "sadness," "frustration," or "being tired," to name a few of the wrong labels I have heard over the years for this particular emotion. Below is a conflict measuring chart, which although simple, has proven to be a great tool. (Many times this person is also suffering from emotional unavailability, and has difficulty sensing, much less admitting, their own needs and emotions.)

Levels of Intensity in Conflict

0 -- No conflict; no fear; no sense of discomfort

1 -- Small disturbance in personal peace levels; no permanent issues

2 -- A sense of agitation; irritation with an event or person; kept within self.

3 -- Stifled anger; subconscious need to protect self

4 -- A greater sense of agitation; voiced irritation with an event or person; sharing anger or frustration.

5 -- Complaint; Visible self-protection; Inner urge to withdraw.

6 -- Recurring concern; Focus of difficulty intrudes on daily thoughts.

7 -- Sensing a need to make a change – driven; sense of urgency (more often)

8 -- Constantly nagging worry; feeling driven to fix something; hyper-responsibility

9 -- Very stressed; no sleep; feeling unequipped to address the concern; overwhelmed

10 -- Feels the end of life as we know it; everything is about to fall apart

Misdirected anger also causes what are known as "somatic," or physical, symptoms of pain within the body. Trigger points are more sensitive, in my own experience with clients, just after periods of stress or conflict.

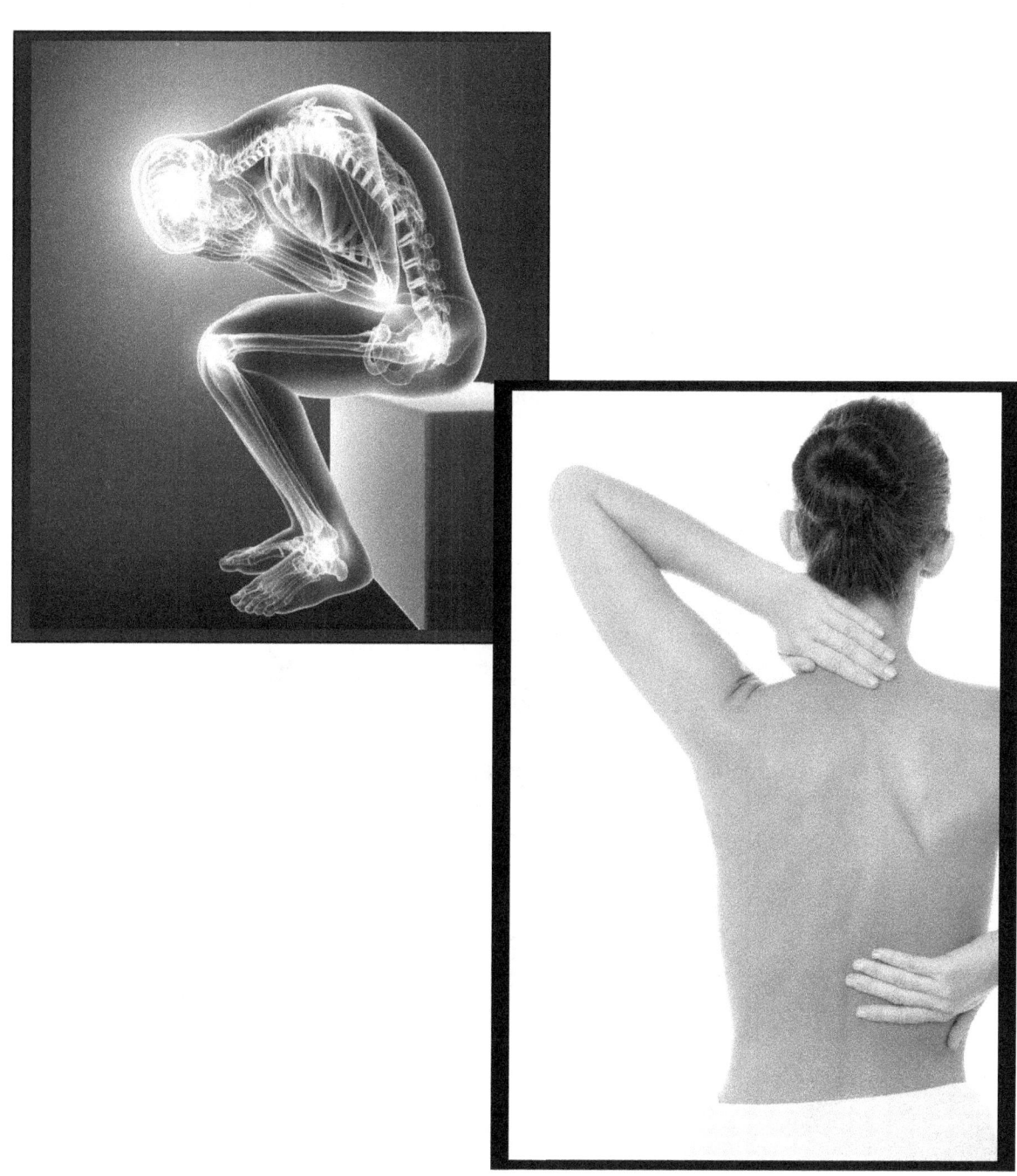

Self-Assessments and Discovery materials

To determine if I'm addicted to habitual anger:

____ I have been known to "overkill" with my anger. Sometimes, my reactions are stronger than they need to be.

____ Other people have told me that they can't always anticipate my responses.

____ Even if I tell myself not to get angry about something, my frustration with people or situations can overtake me.

____ I sometimes can go from really happy to really upset without much warning.

____ Others have told me they're never quite sure how I will respond to a sensitive topic.

____ I feel frustrated or in a hurry most of the time.

____ Its hard to develop close relationships with people.

____ I take my time when asked to believe something. I tend to be skeptical.

____ Somehow I don't seem to learn from past mistakes as well as I should.

Agreeing with four or more of these statements, indicates that Anger has become a habit, and a core element in your identity.

Is Anger A "Safe Place" to me?

1. Do I feel "stronger" when I am angry?

2. Do I get hotheaded and impetuous when I feel angry?

3. How often do I maintain control of my emotions and actions when I become angry?

4. Do I expect to be allowed to "unload" completely when I am angry?

5. Do I have the ability to control my words and actions when my anger is in full gear?

6. What do I think about explosive and impulsive acts when I am angry?

7. Do I let myself hate others, or speak evil words about them?

8. Do I think about how my relationships will survive my angry outburst?

9. Is it possible I am unaware of how deep my angry emotions are, and they surprise me as well as the person I am angry towards?

10. Am I a pouter when things don't go my way?

11. Do I feel my anger cannot be suppressed because it is too powerful to keep to myself?

12. What do I want my relationships to look like in the future? Am I willing to nurture those relationships without utilizing anger to get what I want?

Consider your answers to the above questions. If, in answering the questions, you have discovered that aggressive expressions of anger are either your sense of empowerment, or provide you with a private sense of safety and security; it would be good to seek counsel or look for anger management classes to help you process the wounds that are driving your actions.

Self Assessment – Am I An Angry Person?

How greatly do the following statements apply to you?

1. Impatience comes over me more frequently than I would like.

_____ Yes   _____ No

   If you answered yes, please rate the intensity and frequency

   0   1   2   3   4   5   6   7   8   9   10

   ~~~~

2. I nurture critical thoughts quite easily.

_____ Yes   _____ No

   If you answered yes, please rate the intensity and frequency

   0   1   2   3   4   5   6   7   8   9   10

   ~~~~

3. I feel inwardly annoyed when family and friends do not comprehend my needs.

_____ Yes   _____ No

   If you answered yes, please rate the intensity and frequency

   0   1   2   3   4   5   6   7   8   9   10

   ~~~~

4. Tension mounts within me when I tackle a demanding task.

_____ Yes   ____No

      If you answered yes, please rate the intensity and frequency

      0   1   2   3   4   5   6   7   8   9   10

5. I feel frustrated when I see someone else having fewer struggles than I do.

_____ Yes   ____No

      If you answered yes, please rate the intensity and frequency

      0   1   2   3   4   5   6   7   8   9   10

~~~~~

6. When facing an important event, I may obsessively ponder how I must manage it.

_____ Yes   ____No

      If you answered yes, please rate the intensity and frequency

      0   1   2   3   4   5   6   7   8   9   10

~~~~~

7. Sometimes I walk in another direction to avoid seeing someone I do not like.

_____ Yes   ____No

      If you answered yes, please rate the intensity and frequency

      0   1   2   3   4   5   6   7   8   9   10

~~~~~

8. When discussing a controversial topic, my tone of voice is like to become persuasive.

_____ Yes   _____ No

If you answered yes, please rate the intensity and frequency

0   1   2   3   4   5   6   7   8   9   10

~~~

9. I can accept a person who admits his or her mistakes, but I have a hard time accepting who refuses to admit his or her own weaknesses.

_____ Yes   _____ No

If you answered yes, please rate the intensity and frequency

0   1   2   3   4   5   6   7   8   9   10

~~~

10. When I talk about my irritations, I don't really want to hear an opposite point of view.

_____ Yes   _____ No

If you answered yes, please rate the intensity and frequency

0   1   2   3   4   5   6   7   8   9   10

~~~

11. I do not easily forget when someone does me wrong.

_____ Yes   _____ No

If you answered yes, please rate the intensity and frequency

0   1   2   3   4   5   6   7   8   9   10

~~~

12. When someone confronts me from a misinformed position, I am thinking of my rebuttal as he or she speaks.

_____ Yes   _____ No

      If you answered yes, please rate the intensity and frequency

      0   1   2   3   4   5   6   7   8   9   10

13. Sometimes my discouragement makes me want to quit.

_____ Yes   _____ No

      If you answered yes, please rate the intensity and frequency

      0   1   2   3   4   5   6   7   8   9   10

14. I can be quite aggressive in my business pursuits, or even when I am playing a game just for fun.

_____ Yes   _____ No

      If you answered yes, please rate the intensity and frequency

      0   1   2   3   4   5   6   7   8   9   10

15. I struggle emotionally with the things in life that are not fair.

_____ Yes   _____ No

      If you answered yes, please rate the intensity and frequency

      0   1   2   3   4   5   6   7   8   9   10

16. Although I know it may not be right, I sometimes blame others for my problems.

_____ Yes   _____ No

If you answered yes, please rate the intensity and frequency

0   1   2   3   4   5   6   7   8   9   10

~~~~

17. When someone openly speaks ill of me, my natural response is to think of how I can defend myself.

_____ Yes   _____ No

If you answered yes, please rate the intensity and frequency

0   1   2   3   4   5   6   7   8   9   10

~~~~

18. Sometimes I speak slanderously about a person, not really caring how it may harm his or her reputation.

_____ Yes   _____ No

If you answered yes, please rate the intensity and frequency

0   1   2   3   4   5   6   7   8   9   10

~~~~

19. I may act kindly on the outside while feeling frustrated on the inside.

_____ Yes   _____ No

If you answered yes, please rate the intensity and frequency

0   1   2   3   4   5   6   7   8   9   10

20. Sarcasm is a trait I use in expressing humor.

_____ Yes   ____No

     If you answered yes, please rate the intensity and frequency

     0   1   2   3   4   5   6   7   8   9   10

~~~~~

21. When someone is clearly annoyed with me, I too easily jump into the conflict.

_____ Yes   ____No

     If you answered yes, please rate the intensity and frequency

     0   1   2   3   4   5   6   7   8   9   10

~~~~~

22. At times I struggle with moods of depression or discouragement.

_____ Yes   ____No

     If you answered yes, please rate the intensity and frequency

     0   1   2   3   4   5   6   7   8   9   10

~~~~~

23. I have been known to take an "I don't care" attitude towards the needs of others.

_____ Yes   ____No

     If you answered yes, please rate the intensity and frequency

     0   1   2   3   4   5   6   7   8   9   10

~~~~~

24. When I am in an authority role, I may speak too sternly or act insensitively.

_____ Yes   _____ No

If you answered yes, please rate the intensity and frequency

0   1   2   3   4   5   6   7   8   9   10

~~~~

25. When I displeased with someone, I may shut down any communication or withdraw.

_____ Yes   _____ No

If you answered yes, please rate the intensity and frequency

0   1   2   3   4   5   6   7   8   9   10

~~~~

Self Assessment – Am I Angry?

1. Look back over your answers. How many questions did you answer "yes?" _____

(If you answered more than 10 of the questions with a yes, it indicates an angry life motivation, meaning that anger has a great deal to do with how you approach your life and relationships. Fifteen or more indicate that you are able to recount many instances of anger and disappointments. You are vulnerable to the extreme effects of anger, rage, and explosions, or to guilt, bitterness, and resentment.)

2. Please count up the number of questions you answered "yes," and circled a number lower than 4._____

3. How many questions did you answer "yes," and circle a number higher than 4?_____

(These questions will give you clues as to the habit patterns and learned responses your have developed in regard to your own personal anger management. Think through your answers – where did you see these patterns modeled in your lifetime?)
Please turn to the next page for cumulative scoring.

4. Cumulative Scoring: Please add the numbers of the numbers you circled, and assess your risk for depression with the chart below...

50-100 points   **Reasonably Healthy.** Seasonal moods are normal. We all have stressful moments, and times when we wish we were able to handle our lives more easily. It is important that you take time to refurbish your own heart, and to experience the love and presence of God for yourself. Keep your focus on living a surrendered life, to ward off the temptation to become ruled by angry expressions when they arise.

100-175 points   **Angry and Stressed out.** You have a learned pattern of anger in response to stress in your life. It is usually obvious to those close to you, that you are angry most of the time. Without realizing it, you have probably alienated many of your close relationships, and find yourself without close friends. You are losing contact with your own personal identity, and have allowed anger to become an expected part of your emotional personality. It is time to reassess your life. Pursue counseling for help in learning to change your anger management patterns.

175-250 points   **Red Hot and Rising!** This person is anger driven, and has learned to insulate their life from close relationships through the use of anger. It is possible that physical symptoms are affecting your ability to live life with any form of enjoyment. You could be close to a breakdown of some kind, and should pursue an immediate lifestyle change, as well as seeking counsel for help in changing anger management patterns.

Do I Have an Exploding Type of Anger?

How many of these statements describe your personal method of dealing with anger:

____ I can be direct and forceful when someone does something to frustrate me.

____ When I speak my convictions, my voice becomes increasingly louder.

____ When someone confronts me about a problem, I have no difficulty giving a rebuttal.

____ No one has to guess my opinion; People know where I stand.

____ When something goes wrong, I sometimes concentrate so much on fixing the problem, that I forget to consider others' feelings.

____ It is not unusual for me to become embroiled in disagreements between family members.

____ It is normal for me to repeat myself several times during a verbal disagreement.

____ I find it hard to be quiet about my thoughts and feelings when it is obvious someone is wrong.

____ I have a reputation for being strong willed.

____ I am good at giving advice, even when a person has not asked for advice.

If you marked six or more of these statements, you probably have a pattern of openly aggressive anger. Do you have ongoing struggles with those close to you? Do you spend emotional energy on nonessentials? These answers indicate that you probably deal with a deep insecurity causing you to feel unheard.

Do I Suppress My Anger?

How many of these statements describe your personal method of dealing with anger:

____ It is important to me that I maintain a good image. People don't need to know my problems.

____ I am careful about sharing my problems and frustrations.

____ When I am flustered, I still want people to see me as having things under control.

____ Sometimes I feel trapped by unwanted situations.

____ When someone upsets me, I can let days go by before I bring it up.

____ I wonder if my views are really important or valid at all.

____ It's not unusual for me to become moody or depressed.

____ I have physical ailments on a regular basis. (digestion issues, difficulty sleeping, headaches, etc.)

____ It isn't unusual for me to think of others with resentment. I keep my thoughts to myself.

____ I don't like to talk about difficult or sensitive subjects.

If you agreed with six or more of these statements, it indicates that you have developed a well-established pattern of suppressing your anger. Think it through. Are you uncomfortable with the idea of experiencing or expressing anger?

Am I Passive Aggressive?

How many of these statements describe your personal method of dealing with anger:

_____ When I am frustrated, I become silent, knowing it bothers other people.

_____ I am prone to sulk and pout.

_____ When I don't want to do a project, I will procrastinate. I can be lazy.

_____ When someone asks me if I am frustrated, I will lie and say, "No, everything is fine."

_____ There are times when I am deliberately evasive so others won't bother me.

_____ I sometimes work at projects half-heartedly.

_____ When someone talks to me about my problems, I tend to stare straight ahead, not really wanting to talk, sometimes deliberately obstinate.

_____ I complain about people behind their backs, but resist the opportunity to be open with them face to face.

_____ I have been known to become involved in behind-the-scenes misbehavior.

_____ I enjoy playing practical jokes. I love scaring and/or frustrating others. I have been known to irritate people on purpose, thinking it would be funny to do so.

_____ I sometimes refuse to do someone a favor, just wanting to see if it irritates them.

If you agreed with six or more of these statements, it indicates that you have developed a pattern of expressing your anger in a quiet manner which gives you control, but still providing the least amount of personal vulnerability. You have learned to use subtle sabotage to "get even," or make your point. This is a battle for superiority. It is passive aggression.

How Persistent is Pride in my Life Attitude?

How many of these statements describe your personal perspective?

_____ I wonder sometimes why people are not as considerate as they should be.

_____ It really bothers me when someone is insensitive towards me.

_____ I can become impatient or edgy when people are incompetent.

_____ If I sense respect coming my way, it makes me feel good.

_____ I am known to have a strong personality.

_____ Sometimes I fantasize what life would be like if I could have ideal circumstances.

_____ When someone I know experiences something good, my initial response is to wish the same thing to happen in my own life.

_____ It makes me angry when another person does not receive my opinions well.

_____ I avoid making personal or private disclosures if possible.

_____ When I am in a social circle, I feel responsible to maintain a perfect reputation, even if I have to cover my reputation with a half-truth.

_____ I would prefer to avoid disclosures of a personal nature.

If you agreed with five or more of these statements, it indicates that pride has gained a foothold on your emotions. Anger is inevitable.

How Pervasive is Fear in my Life Approach?

How many of these statements describe your personal perspective?

____ I have been told that I don't receive other's criticism or feedback very well.

____ I am uncomfortable when I am in a situation when I am not in control of things.

____ Sometimes I use humor to redirect a conversation I am uncomfortable with.

____ There are parts of my personality no one knows about.

____ I am affected by the moods of other people.

____ I am careful about my emotions. I don't like to share intimate feelings or thoughts.

____ I tend to let my frustrations grow, and I think about them. It is hard to let go and relax.

____ I worry about what people think of me than most people would realize.

____ I have told lies in the past to keep others from seeing or discovering my personal flaws.

____ When someone is clearly angry, I habitually seek to protect myself.

____ I worry more about my public image than most people would suspect.

Each of these statements represents a subtle form of fear. If you agreed with six or more of these statements, it indicates that you probably struggle too often with this emotion, and in turn you bring frustration and anger into your world.

Section Five.
Required Choices to Heal

Practical Ways to Diffuse Personal Anger

1. Choose not to be ruled by pride. Pride is preoccupied with self, expecting to be put in the place of highest importance. Pride is a actually self-rule, rather than Holy Spirit rule in the life. Determine to choose humility as a life approach. Repent for pride, and allow the Father to put your life in perspective with His plan and purposes, rather than your own.

2. Choose to be others focused. What are the needs of others? How could you help to serve them?

3. Choose to accept limits, in your behavior and in your relationships. Accept the fact that others are different from yourself. In making the decision to serve others, make that decision from your heart, as a life choice – do it with all of your being; turning away from the anger that has been so destructive to others and to yourself. This kind of choice is not a repressing of your emotions, but rather a healthy choice to change.

4. Let go of the fear of not being in control. Spend some time in worship, and allow the Presence of God to invade your heart, touching on the hurt underneath the anger you are feeling.

5. Review the following healthy life approach statements:

   a. I would like to be remembered as a person who is easy to approach and get to know.

   b. I would like to be known as a helpful and considerate person.

   c. I can be patient when people do things to irritate me.

   d. I can relax, and learn to have peace in my heart when I relate to other people.

   e. Spending time with people is a great way to develop friendships and maintain them.

f. Problems don't have to be resolved on my timetable.

g. If I expect others to accept me with my weaknesses, I can accept their weaknesses as well.

h. I can relax when In feel time compressed.

i. I would like to be known as someone who is a good friend and encourager.

j. I want to become someone who notices the good things in other people's character development.

l. I really want to experience laughing with my friends.

m. I really am tired of having to protect myself by masking who I really am when I am with other people.

n. I don't want my focus to be on the negative. I want to focus on the positive.

o. I want to be less self-centered.

How To Develop Healthy Anger Management

1. Admit that you have an anger problem, and take responsibility for the damages your unhealthy expressions of anger have caused in your own life, and in the lives of others.

2. Begin to notice your personal method of dealing with recognized personal anger. Where did you learn to react this way?

3. How would you like to handle your anger in a more healthy way?

4. Seek the help of a friend or counselor who can help you gain an objective viewpoint of your anger responses. In the process, you might encounter pain from past experiences, which have been "covered over" by your unknowing protective choice to become angry.

5. Choose to receive the unconditional love of Father God, even when you have been angry, or have failed. Allow your heart to accept the value He has communicated He places on your life.

6. Develop a friendship with someone else. Choose to let them into your life on an unconditional level.

7. Work on a plan to respond differently when you are angry than you presently respond. Perhaps write it down, and set small goals to help yourself achieve this change.

8. Begin keeping track of your emotions, by journaling your thoughts and feelings. The purpose is to help you become more self-aware without being selfish.

9. Consider changing patterns in your life to become more healthy in relationships. Consider Philippians 2:3-4, Ephesians 4:28-32, and I Corinthians 13:4-7. How do these Scriptures describe relationships that function differently than your do at the present time?

10. Choose to slow down in your responding when you are completely angry. Try to control the personal impulse to speak your mind or "unload" regarding injustices you feel, until you are able to let go of the "heat" in your emotions. Then, try to discuss the issue without anger.

11. Find something constructive to do, to help you redirect your emotions into a altered direction. Here are some suggestions:

go for a run	clean a room
organize a closet	work-out at the gym
listen to soft music	breathe deeply
sit alone in a dark room	pray
watch a funny movie	read a joke book
call a friend	play a game on the computer

12. Realize that your anger has its roots in one of three things: fear, frustration, or hurt. Ask yourself these questions: "Why am I hurt?" "What am I frustrated about" "What am I afraid of?" When anger surfaces, try focusing on the emotions that are indicated below the anger. What is the root cause? Then, choose to surrender those deep emotions to the Spirit of God, allowing Him to work in your life.

Section Six.
The Bible on Anger

Notes to Consider

1. There are times when it is healthy to address concerns about our personal worth, needs, and convictions. When this process takes place in a healthy manner, it keeps inward doors of the heart open for ongoing positive relationship and mutual sharing. When the heart's doors are closed, improper expressions of Anger present themselves.

2. Learning the skill of maintaining healthy boundaries kindly is a way of practicing this healthy assertion.

3. When we feel unloved, we learn to be dependent upon the responses of other people, to enable us to feel loved. All of our security becomes based on outer communication and motivations, rather than on the Spirit of God, flowing through the inner man.

4. According to Ephesians 4:26-32, there **is a difference between being assertive, and being aggressive. Healthy assertion is not unhealthy aggression. When we are weak in an area of living, the tendency of the flesh is to substitute aggression for assertiveness.**

    This substitution indicates several things about our personal discipleship:
    We are unable to trust the voice of the Spirit of God for direction. We experience the crippling effects of self-doubt, and live with unbalanced dependencies?

5. Spiritual health must be the first thing we establish if we desire to be healthy people. When we do not establish spiritual health, we learn to justify living our lives driven by our carnalities and flesh.

6. According to Romans 8:8, those who live their lives in the flesh cannot discover how to please God. For that reason, let's look at the description of the flesh, and what its elements represent when it comes to living our lives before God. The flesh has its base in Pride.

7. Based on Galatians 5:19-23, let's look at a comparison of the evidences of the flesh and the fruit of the Holy Spirit.

FLESH	HOLY SPIRIT
Adultery, fornication,	Love, joy, peace
Uncleanness, lewdness	patience, (longsuffering)
Idolatry, sorcery, hatred	kindness, goodness,
Contentions, jealousies	faithfulness, gentleness,
Outbursts of anger, revelries	self-control
Selfish ambitions, envy, murders	
Dissensions, heresies, drunkenness	

8. According to Philippians 4:8, the believer is encouraged and instructed to learn to develop the skill of a contemplative mind; allowing the Holy Spirit to allow us to see situations, people and circumstances from His perspective.

9. When we come under another person's control, we feel angry, because we deny our God-given identity, in order to gain that person's approval.

10. According to the account of Cain and Abel in Genesis 4:1-8, How does God see our Anger?

Cain and Abel	God told Cain that sin was crouched waiting at the door When he was angry, and that he would have to master it. But Cain chose the anger, and allowed it to rule him.

11. According to James 1:20, the wrath of man does not work the righteousness of God. That means there is no such thing as "righteous indignation."

12. We sometimes sabotage our own lives, by just letting anger lead us.

13. Is anger always bad? See Mark 3:1-5... Aren't some things are worth being angry over.

14. Stubbornness and resistance against the Father's plan stirred Jesus' anger.

15. Negative angry expression is misdirected Passion.

16. When we care about what God cares about, anger is justifiable.

17. Unhealthy anger expressions take things into our own hands.
18. Unhealthy anger expressions elevate us in our own minds above others-- Attitudes of superiority fuel anger, because they are based on pride. They close off the heart to the voice of the Holy Spirit.

19. Abba Father's instructions confronted Peter's traditions; he had every opportunity to become angry. Instead however, Peter chose obedience. Peter and Cornelius – Acts 10:34 – Peter gave

20. What does the Bible say?   Proverbs 14:17 – slow to anger

21. Based on Ephesians 4:26, we are instructed not to sin when we are angry.

22. Based on Ephesians 4:31, we are told to put anger away from us

23. Since anger is an evidence of powerlessness, when we are expressing our anger, it is important that we remember that the Lord's power is made perfect in what?

    (our weakness)   see II Corinthians 12:9

24. A quick connection from Fear to Anger -- - When we are angry, we many times cling to our anger, not wanting to admit that we have chosen to allow it to continue to torment us, and we blame others for the fact that it is present in our lives at all.

The Broken Soul; How it Relates to the Levels of Communication and Relationship

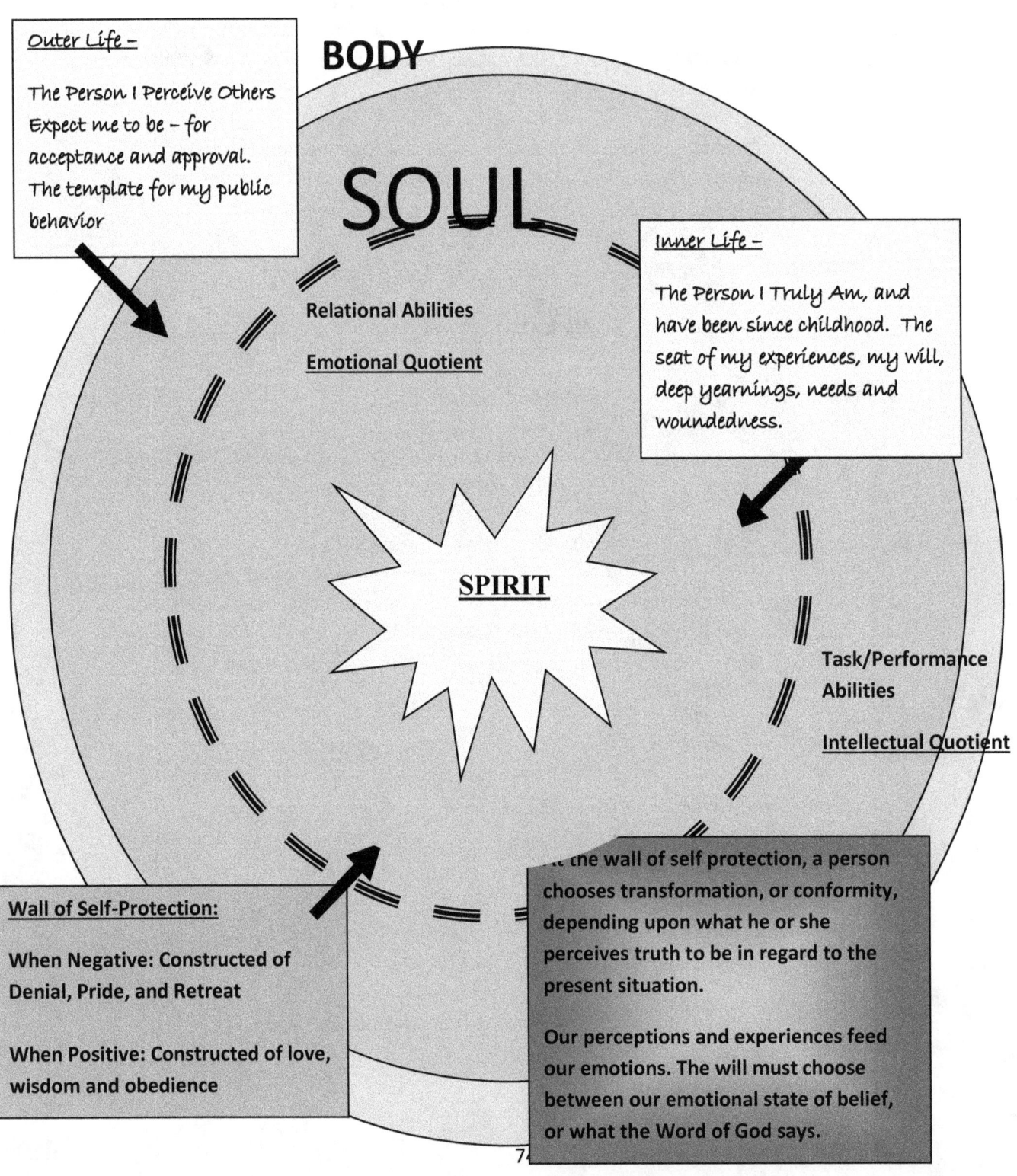

Outer Life –

The Person I Perceive Others Expect me to be – for acceptance and approval. The template for my public behavior

BODY

SOUL

Relational Abilities

Emotional Quotient

Inner Life –

The Person I Truly Am, and have been since childhood. The seat of my experiences, my will, deep yearnings, needs and woundedness.

SPIRIT

Task/Performance Abilities

Intellectual Quotient

Wall of Self-Protection:

When Negative: Constructed of Denial, Pride, and Retreat

When Positive: Constructed of love, wisdom and obedience

At the wall of self protection, a person chooses transformation, or conformity, depending upon what he or she perceives truth to be in regard to the present situation.

Our perceptions and experiences feed our emotions. The will must choose between our emotional state of belief, or what the Word of God says.

The Blindness of Pride

II Corinthians 4:3-4   *But even if our gospel is veiled, it is veiled to those who are perishing, whose minds the god of this age has blinded, who do not believe, lest the light of the gospel of the glory of Christ, who is the image of God, should shine on them.*

I John 2:10-11   *He who loves his brother abides in the light, and there is no cause for stumbling in him. But he who hates his brother is in darkness and walks in darkness, and does not know where he is going, because the darkness has blinded his eyes.*

Pride, simply put, is the unwillingness to allow God to protect and take care of us.

Qualities of Pride – Pride refuses to acknowledge or admit need. Pride makes comparisons, presumes, rebels and seeks to be independent, while at the same time, demanding that everyone in its sphere of influence come into its way of thinking. It will not associate in vulnerable community. It blames, criticizes, and places its own opinion above anyone else's. It is the root of selfishness, placing its own needs and wants above those of anyone else. It seeks to be understood, rather than to understand. It seeks to rule. It seeks to control. It demands to be heard. In its most raw form, it is denial. In its inverted form, it takes the form of self-pity, victimization, and accusation, continually stating that it has been misunderstood.

All demonic torment has its root in pride.

James 4:6   *But He gives more grace. Therefore He says: " God resists the proud, but gives grace to the humble."*

Phrases Pride Will Not Say –

1. **I was wrong. Dead wrong."** (without accompanying explanations or excuses.)

    When humility makes this statement, it does so without explanations or excuses. It also admits truth. Jesus wants us to live in the truth.

    Psalm 15:1- 2   *LORD, who may abide in Your tabernacle? Who may dwell in Your holy hill? He who walks uprightly, and works righteousness, and speaks the truth in his heart;*

    Ephesians 4:15   *that we should no longer be children, tossed to and fro and carried about with every wind of doctrine, by the trickery of men, in the cunning craftiness of deceitful plotting, but, speaking the truth in love, may grow up in all things into Him who is the head—Christ—*

    Psalm 51:6   *Behold, You desire truth in the inward parts, and in the hidden part You will make me to know wisdom.*

    III John 1:2-4   *Beloved, I pray that you may prosper in all things and be in health, just as your soul prospers. For I rejoiced greatly when brethren came and testified of the truth that is in you, just as you walk in the truth. I have no greater joy than to hear that my children walk in truth.*

2. **"I am responsible."** (without accompanying rationalizations and blame).

    When humility makes this statement, it does so without seeking to be understood. Rather, it seeks to make things right, and bring restitution.

    James 4:6   *But He gives more grace. Therefore He says: " God resists the proud, but gives grace to the humble."*

3. **"I am willing to experience the consequences of my actions. I have earned them."** (without bringing justice arguments)

When humility makes this statement, it makes no comparisons with other's behaviors, or with regard to fairness. It is enough for the character quality of humility that the issues be settled on their on regard, without expecting others to facilitate or protect them.

Hebrews 12:5-6 And you have forgotten the exhortation which speaks to you as to sons: " My son, do not despise the chastening of the LORD, nor be discouraged when you are rebuked by Him; For whom he LORD loves He chastens, and scourges every son whom He receives."

4. **"I need Jesus."** (no self made solutions)

When humility makes this statement, it acknowledges its own need for Jesus, without making statements or judgments as to the behavior of others, or of their relational treatment. It seeks only to correct and make right its own person.

Psalm 10:4 The wicked in his proud countenance does not seek God; God is in none of his thoughts.

5. **"I can't fix myself."** (without knowledge arguments)
6. **"I don't know the answer."**

When humility makes this statement, it does so without making a defensive statement about what it knows, or what it has held on to as truth. I realizes that its needs help, and receives it willingly.

James 4:16-17 But now you boast in your arrogance. All such boasting is evil. Therefore, to him who knows to do good and does not do it, to him it is sin.

7. **"I trust God more than I trust myself, and that's wrong. I choose to trust God."** (without self reliance, or independence)
8. **"I surrender."**

When humility makes this statement, it recognizes personal need for accountability, discipline, and training. It recognizes that it is not its own authority, and opens observation those inner places of the heart where pride has ruled.

Jeremiah 49:16 *Your fierceness has deceived you, the pride of your heart, O you who dwell in the clefts of the rock, who hold the height of the hill! Though you make your nest as high as the eagle, I will bring you down from there," says the LORD*

Romans 9:19-21 *You will say to me then, "Why does He still find fault? For who has resisted His will?" But indeed, O man, who are you to reply against God? Will the thing formed say to him who formed it, "Why have you made me like this?" Does not the potter have power over the clay, from the same lump to make one vessel for honor and another for dishonor?*

9. **"I need to change."** (without self-defense)

When humility makes this statement, it stands in the place of security in the love of Father God, knowing that He will make things right, and that He will take care of how we are perceived, understood and known, as long as we stay in alignment with Him, and seek to keep our carnal flesh in check.

Proverbs 16:17-20 *The highway of the upright is to depart from evil; He who keeps his way preserves his soul. Pride goes before destruction, and a haughty spirit before a fall. Better to be of a humble spirit with the lowly, than to divide the spoil with the proud. He who heeds the word wisely will find good, and whoever trusts in the LORD, happy is he.*

10. **"I repent. I was wrong. I'm sorry. Will you forgive me?"** (without self preservation attitudes)

When humility makes this statement, it receives and acknowledges responsibility for wrong behaviors, attitudes and treatments of others. It does not seek to hide behind a need to be seen as "right," or "in control."

II Corinthians 7:9-10 *Now I rejoice, not that you were made sorry, but that your sorrow led to repentance. For you were made sorry in a godly manner, that you might suffer loss from us in nothing. For godly sorrow produces repentance leading to salvation, not to be regretted; but the sorrow of the world produces death.*

11. **"I need to be taught more than I need to be understood."**

When humility makes this statement, it opens itself to others in a chain of command, asking those people to speak into the life for health and growth. It receives correction and teaching, and applies what it is taught, in order to bring about health and growth, and seeing change occur in the life.

Galatians 6:3 *For if anyone thinks himself to be something, when he is nothing, he deceives himself.*

12. **"The truth is more important than anything I feel, or whatever image I portray."** (with nothing to hide – no secret living)

When humility makes this statement it is acknowledging that the images we seek to portray are false, and that they never allow us to put God first. Humility is willing to live an honest life, without seeking to make impressions of success, achievement, financial status, or intellectual accomplishments. It is most concerned with straightforward relationships and honest living before God.

II Timothy 3:1-5 *But know this, that in the last days perilous times will come: For men will be lovers of themselves, lovers of money, boasters, proud, blasphemers, disobedient to parents, unthankful, unholy, unloving, unforgiving, slanderers, without self-control, brutal, despisers of good, traitors, headstrong, haughty, lovers of pleasure rather than lovers of God, having a form of godliness but denying its power. And from such people turn away!*

Anybody can become angry —

that is easy, but to be angry with the right person

and to the right degree and at the right time

and for the right purpose, and in the right way —

that is not within everybody's power and is not easy."

— Aristotle

Section Seven.
Scriptural Prayer and Supportive Materials.

General Prayer for Freedom

Father God, I acknowledge you as my heavenly Father. I understand and believe what the Word of God says about your nature.

Earthly men may hate me, but You love me. Earthly men may seek to violate and control me, but you will never violate my will. Earthly men may have abused me, but I know that there is no end to your mercy and love for me. I know that you desire to make my paths straight, and to bless me. You do not reward me according to my sins, but according to Your own righteousness.

I have a purpose in Your eyes, and You want me to know and understand that purpose. You want to be my strength when I am weak. You want to be my refuge and to deliver me from all evil. You want me to trust in You and be helped.

So, Father God, I choose today, to surrender to Yom will for my life. I choose to be obedient to You. I choose to obey the authority figures you have put into my life. I know they must give account for my soul.

Lord Jesus, I acknowledge and accept Your gift of life for me. Thank you for the provision of your Blood, which is eternal and all powerful, and has no limits in its availability to me. I apply that Blood to my heart and my life. I repent for allowing the influences and powers of darkness to acquire my allegiance. Please forgive me for listening to those voices and giving in to them. Please wash away the false security which has deceived my heart into forsaking You when seeking love and comfort.

Please melt away those chains which I have allowed to overtake my heart. I repent for seeking comfort and escape anywhere but through Your provision of love for me. I turn away from self-reliance and trusting my own flesh, and the flesh of others to guide me. I choose to trust You. I choose to trust Your word to be the complete counsel for my life.

I choose to disregard any suspicious nature which the enemy of my soul, the devil, uses against me to accuse or condemn those You have put in my path to help and bless me and bring me into freedom.

I surrender my desire to be in control of my deliverance. I choose to follow with an open and listening heart.

Father, I confess my fear to you. I am afraid of being violated when my walls are taken down. I am afraid the process of destruction will begin all over again. But I know these are threats from the kingdom of darkness, and so I ask for your Perfect love to cast out fear in me in regard to my freedom. Please be the strength of my life and my shield. Please be the strong high tower into which I can run for safety. You are my Helper.

I want to become the person you created me to be.

I acknowledge you as the Restorer of my soul, and I recognize that Satan has stolen from me my purpose, he has lied to me and brought death and destruction to my heart, life and mind.

I hate him with a perfect hatred. I will not allow demonic voices to give me a false sense of security and identity. I choose to hear Your voice, Father God. Please speak to me.

Holy Spirit, I release You within my heart, and I give you full permission to make my life and person a holy and pure vessel for your habitation.

Thank you Lord that you love me. I am your child. I choose Your way.

Prayer to help in Releasing Forgiveness

Father God, thank you for your love for me. I know that you love me unconditionally. I choose to walk in Your ways.

Thank you for the gift of your Son, Who died so that I might live forever.

Father, I choose to forgive everyone who has knowingly and unknowingly inflicted hurts and bruises upon my life.

With my will, I will forgive, and I trust You to fill my heart with your love and the feelings of forgiveness in the days to come.

Father, I choose to release my rights to hold on to these hurts and bruises. I choose to confess them to you, and allow you to be the vindicator and Healer of my Heart.

Thank you for your peace. In Jesus' name, Amen.

To Overcome Anger

*"He that is slow to anger is better than the mighty;
and he that rules his own spirit
than he that takes a city."* Proverbs 16:32

Anger is a secondary emotion. It erupts to the surface of a life when there is unresolved pain, or un-forgiven hurt in a person's life. In smaller issues, anger can be easily dealt with, by making a choice to forgive the person who has hurt you, and laying the right of keeping of life-accounts at the feet of Father God. In I Corinthians 13, we are told that love keeps no record of wrongs, and in Romans 5:5, God has promised to shed His love abroad in our hearts. When we respond in anger, we are short-circuiting our chance to love a person with the love of God. We are keeping record of wrongs.

In larger issues, anger must be confronted aggressively. It is an area to which demonic forces seek to attach themselves, and it is usually accompanied by violence, fear and/or depression. This type of violent anger can usually be traced to an open door, which was created in a person's childhood, through abuse, neglect, or example. Many times, a person in the cycle of the bondage of anger will seek to escape their inner pain by seeking refuge in alcohol, drugs, or another addictive behavior.

Anger is an emotion, which must be dealt with quickly and aggressively, giving no place to the devil, for it works like acid upon the human soul, quickly developing habit patterns.

It will help to pray in this manner:

Father God, I confess to you my anger. It is my choice to repent for allowing anger to develop in my heart. My wrath does not work your righteousness. I ask for your forgiveness for those places where I have sinned in my anger. Please develop within me the ability to be slow to anger.

Please give me a forgiving spirit. I choose to forgive those who have hurt me, and I I bring you my heart. I understand that I must forgive, in order for your forgiveness to be fully released in my own life. Please heal my life, and release me from the cycle of the bondage of anger. I choose to let go of my right to be angry. It is the desire of my heart to be able to have Holy Spirit-led control over my own spirit.

I acknowledge that Your Word says that vengeance is Yours and You will repay. I choose not to take these hurts personally, but to recognize that those who have hurt me are operating out of their own pain and bondage. In making this choice, I

understand that your Word says that You will undertake in these things on my behalf. I will wait for your timing in making these things right. Thank you for loving me.
Father God, it is my choice to humble myself before You, and to allow you to rebuild the walls of my soul and personality. Anger is not the definition of your purpose for my life. Please make me what you want me to be. I choose to yield to you. Please develop the Holy Spirit's fruit of unconditional love, gentleness and kindness in my heart.

I choose to seek Your Will and Way for my life. I open the door of my soul to your love for me. Please wash away everything that stands in the way of my receiving your perfect and unconditional love.

Lord, I confess that Your Word says that my wrath does not work your righteousness. I confess that anger rests in the bosom of fools. It is my desire to be free and dedicated to you in every area of my life. Therefore, I choose to turn away from anger.

Anger, I will not serve you any longer. Rage, you have no hold on me. Violence, I will not be your slave. I belong to the Lord God of Hosts. The Blood of the Lamb of God is against you, and is applied to the door of my life. You have no authority to, speak to me, because I choose to remove every legal right I have given you to deal in my life. Anger, you cannot speak into my life, or influence me, because my hope is in the Lord Jesus Christ and His work upon the Cross for me. I do not even have to fight this battle, for the battle is not mine, but it belongs to the Lord. You have been defeated by the death of the Son of God, and I will not give you place any longer.

Proverbs 16:32	Proverbs 19:11	Proverbs 25:28	Proverbs 29:22-23
Ecclesiastes 7:9	Ephesians 4:26-27	Ephesians 4:31-32	James 1:19-20
Romans 12:19	Proverbs 15: 1		

For more Biblically based materials to utilize as a Scriptural foundation for helping others, please refer to our other "A Christian Counselor's Primer on..." series handbooks.

What Proverbs teaches us about Anger

1. **Proverbs 14:17**   A quick-tempered *man* acts foolishly, and a man of wicked intentions is hated. *(People who are habitually angry make mistakes)*

2. **Proverbs 25:28**   Whoever *has* no rule over his own spirit is *like* a city broken down, without walls. *(People who are habitually angry are vulnerable)*

3. **Proverbs 29:22**   An angry man stirs up strife, and a furious man abounds in transgression.   *(People who are habitually angry can't keep it to themselves.)*

4. **Proverbs 16:32**   *He who is* slow to anger *is* better than the mighty, and he who rules his spirit than he who takes a city. *(To control unhealthy anger makes us mighty.)*

5. **Proverbs 19:19**   *A man of* great wrath will suffer punishment; for if you rescue *him*, you will have to do it again. *(Habitual anger Is recurring, and requires rescue from more level headed people.)*

6. **Proverbs 22:24-25**   Make no friendship with an angry man, and with a furious man do not go, lest you learn his ways and set a snare for your soul. *(People who are habitually angry are to be treated like they have a contagious disease).*

7. **Proverbs 15:13**   A merry heart makes a cheerful countenance, but by sorrow of the heart the spirit is broken. *(What is in the heart shows on the countenance/demeanor).*

8. **Proverbs 4:23**   Keep your heart with all diligence, for out of it *spring* the issues of life. *(Guard what you allow to come out of your heart.)*

9. **Proverbs 15:23**   A man has joy by the answer of his mouth, and a word *spoken* in due season, how good *it is*! *(What we allow to come out of our mouth will determine what we feel.)*

10. **Proverbs 12:25**   Anxiety in the heart of man causes depression, but a good word makes it glad.

11. **Proverbs 20:22** Do not say, "I will recompense evil"; Wait for the LORD, and He will save you. *(When we take control in anger, we push Father out of the picture.)*

12. **Proverbs 19:11** The discretion of a man makes him slow to anger, and his glory *is* to overlook a transgression. *(It is wise to determine what is worth being angry over, taking action.)*

13. **Proverbs 17:14** The beginning of strife *is like* releasing water; therefore stop contention before a quarrel starts. *(Once habitual anger is unleashed, it is like the breaking of a dam – out of control and causing destruction.)*

14. **Proverbs 3:5-7** Trust in the LORD with all your heart, and lean not on your own understanding; In all your ways acknowledge Him, and He shall direct your paths. Do not be wise in your own eyes; fear the LORD and depart from evil. *(Don't think you have it all together – let the Lord have the places you don't understand. He will bring solution and direction.)*

Suggested Reading List – Anger Issues

1. **Angry Men and the Women who Love Them** by Paul Hegstrom. (ISBN: 978-0834121522) Published by Beacon Hill Press of Kansas City, 2004. 152 pages.

2. **Broken Children, Grown Up Pain** by Paul Hegstrom. (ISBN: 978-0834122512) Published by Beacon Hill Press of Kansas City, 2006) 152 pages

3. **Anger: Handling a Powerful Emotion in a Healthy Way** by Gary D Chapman. (ISBN: 978-1881273882) Published by Northfield Publishing; 2007) 240 pages

4. *The Anger Trap: Free Yourself from the Frustrations that Sabotage Your Life by Les Carter and Frank Minirth (ISBN: 978-0787968809) Published by Jossey-Bass, 2004. 224 Pages.*

5. *The Dance of Anger: A Woman's Guide to Changing the Patterns of Intimate Relationships by Harriet Lerner (ISBN:978-006074104X) Published by Perennial Currents, 20th Anniversary Edition, 2005. 239 pages.*

6. **Why Does He Do That? Inside the Minds of Angry and Controlling Men** by Lundy Bancroft. (ISBN 978-0425191651) Published by Berkley Books, Reprint edition, 2003. 432 pages

More from Awakened to Grow…

Be sure to complete your set of ATG's handbooks from **A Christian Counselor's Primer On…** series. Titles include Depression, Communication, Fear and Anxiety, Processing Grief, and many more!

Each reference tool contains charts and assessments for personal discovery and development. Recorded teaching sessions are available for each handbook. Just contact us through our website! Handbooks vary in length and are priced at $20 each. *(Published, 2014)*

Elements of Identity Formation – Outlines and charts help the student understand the process of emotional and spiritual identity formation. Especially helpful for all those who struggle with understanding how to experience the love of God on a personal level. Recorded teaching sessions are available for each handbook. Just contact us through our website!
Workbook is available on amazon.com and lulu.com

 **journey – a novel; The real story of a girl called "Magdalene."** A compelling weaving of historical and Biblical events, this painstakingly researched account of the life of Mary Magdalene will surprise you in how it relates to our present culture and your own personal history.   504 pages *(2nd edition) $33.50 (MSRP) (Published, 2009 & 2014) Available at amazon.com and/or lulu.com*

Secrets for Relational Living -- For every person who wants to experience healthy relationships! This 8 session class can be studied individually or with a group. Video sessions of the teachings are available through our website. Especially helpful for all those who feel inwardly insecure in successfully communicating and relating to others.
Available on amazon.com and lulu.com

The Chronicles of Hausse – Book One; The Trouble with Dragons -- An allegorical adventure, set in the mystical land of Hausse; where Lightbearers and Demons can be seen and danger lurks around every corner! Written to explain the spiritual realm to middle school and high school aged students, this book has received rave reviews from readers from 8 to 80!
368 pages $22.00 (MSRP) (Published, 2012) *Available at amazon.com and/or lulu.com*

For a more complete listing, please check out our listings on Amazon.com and lulu.com. Please also see our worship/music resources on iTunes.

www.ingramcontent.com/pod-product-compliance
Lightning Source LLC
Chambersburg PA
CBHW080348170426
43194CB00014B/2725